Completing Your Thesis or Dissertation

Professors Share Their Techniques and Strategies

Fred Pyrczak, Editor

California State University, Los Angeles

Pyrczak Publishing

P.O. Box 39731 • Los Angeles, CA 90039

Although the author and publisher have made every effort to ensure the accuracy and completeness of information contained in this book, we assume no responsibility for errors, inaccuracies, omissions, or any inconsistency herein. Any slights of people, places, or organizations are unintentional.

Editorial assistance provided by Brenda Koplin, Cheryl Alcorn, Sharon Young, Elaine Fuess, and Randall R. Bruce.

Cover design by Robert Kibler and Larry Nichols.

Printed in the United States of America.
10 9 8 7 6 5 4 3 2 1   DOC   07 06 05 04 03 02 01 00

ISBN 1-884585-21-3

Introduction

Preparing a thesis or dissertation is a culminating activity for graduate students. In the ideal, it should be a straightforward outgrowth of a student's previous experiences in graduate school. However, many students are intimidated by the quantitative differences between a typical term project in a graduate-level class and a thesis or dissertation (e.g., a dissertation involves more faculty members, requires a more comprehensive review of the literature, and is substantially longer than a typical class project).

Arguably, the qualitative differences are even more problematic for many students. A thesis or dissertation is what is known in educational circles as a "performance test," a test in which the examinee performs a sequence of steps to create a product or demonstrate a set of skills. Unlike most other tests students have taken (including term projects), the criteria for passing this test are highly subjective (e.g., judgments need to be made about the originality and scientific merit of the research purposes) and are subject to negotiation (e.g., students may try to convince committee members of the merits of various aspects of their performance).

The problem is compounded by the fact that the thesis or dissertation "test" has many novel elements. For example, the time frame is exceedingly long, three professors (not just one) need to be satisfied, and students must work one-on-one with their committee chair and other members of their committee without the structure of a classroom environment.

Quite understandably, taking a novel test with high standards for quantity and highly subjective standards for quality is cause enough for considerable concern, if not alarm. Knowing that a thesis or dissertation is one of the most important "tests" a student will ever take causes additional anxiety for many.

Confronted with this complex set of circumstances, many students procrastinate, avoid, and mentally block. A distressingly large number never complete their theses and dissertations, including many who fail to complete even the initial stages such as writing an acceptable proposal or prospectus.

What's the Solution?

The philosophy underlying this book is that there is no one solution or set of solutions for solving the problem outlined above. This is true largely because each thesis or dissertation has many unique elements (e.g., a unique topic that poses its own design problems; unique committee members, each of whom may have different expectations and standards; and a unique student with his or her own learning styles, work habits, and personal needs).

However, it is safe to say that most students undertaking a thesis or dissertation need support and guidance. The existing books on preparing a thesis or dissertation tend to provide proscriptive guidance of a sequential nature (e.g., set a deadline for completing Step 1, follow Step 2, and so on). These are helpful for most students. However, this book is of a different genre. It is a compilation of tips, techniques, and strategies *that have worked for other people and are expressed in their own words*—not a sequential, one-size-fits-all prescription. From this compilation, students should judiciously select those contributions that seem most promising while keeping in mind that what worked for one person might not be effective for another person in a different situation.

Suggestions for Using This Book

Ideally, graduate students should read this book before they start the thesis or dissertation process. As they read it, they should make comments on their personal reactions in the "Notes" spaces provided throughout the book. Pages with important comments should be noted with self-adhesive flags or small Post-It® sheets for later reference or possible transcription to a master document.

In a thesis or dissertation class, the contributions in this book may be selected by the professor or by students for class discussion. Possible topics for discussion are: Which contributions are most promising for each phase of the thesis or dissertation process? Do any of the suggestions seem nonproductive? Which contributions are the most creative or unique? Which of the suggestions is each student planning to follow?

Navigating Through This Book

Students who are just starting their graduate school program might simply read this book from cover to cover, noting important points to which they might want to refer later.

For students who have already begun the thesis or dissertation process and need help with only selected aspects of the process, the running sidebars throughout this book and the Guide to Selected Contributions that immediately follows this introduction will assist in locating relevant material.

For those who need a bit of comic relief, note that humorous and tongue-in-cheek contributions are indicated in the sidebars with (**Ha!**) and are classified in the Guide to Selected Contributions under the heading "Humor."

A Note on the History of This Book

Pyrczak Publishing contracted with an author to write a book to help students with the thesis/dissertation process. I thought it would be a good idea to get suggestions from other professors that might be incorporated into the book. To solicit them, we inserted a flyer with the examination and desk copies of books that we routinely ship. Within a short time, we had collected a large number of responses from professors. Reviewing them, I realized that much would be lost by synthesizing and summarizing them into a single author's proscriptive book. The raw material, it seemed, was worthy of being in its own book, especially since the material would be read by advanced graduate students who could easily handle the free form of an "in-their-own-words" book.

In editing the book, my first temptation was to put the contributions in order, starting with those that dealt with the first steps in the process, then with subsequent steps. However, because many of the contributions deal with various steps that are not always in sequence, they would need to be broken up into pieces and scattered throughout the book. Breaking them up and imposing structure on them would take away the uniqueness of the material and make it difficult for readers to see which topics each contributor deemed important enough to write about in a single contribution. In the end, I decided to let you, the reader, impose your own structure.

Communicating with Me

I would be thrilled to hear from you. What did you like most about this book? How could it be improved? Most of all, I would like to hear about your success in completing a thesis or dissertation. Also, contributions from both students and professors for a second edition of this book will be welcome. My address is on the title page of this book.

Fred Pyrczak

O cat

Contributions

Continued →

Contribution 1

Hema Ramanathan
Butler University

Classified Advertisement

Wanted: A Shadow Researcher!

Responsibilities:

- Meet for coffee/lunch at least once a week for an hour.
- Look at my data as I gather it.
- Comment on the data, the instrument, the analysis. (No, you don't write my dissertation for me!)
- The job lasts while I complete my dissertation (at least a year!).

Required qualifications:

- A fellow graduate student.
- Someone with whom I am likely to take a couple of classes.
- Someone not necessarily in my major area of interest but in the same discipline. (I am an education major and the dissertation process in the sciences or engineering is too different from mine!).
- Someone who will have the time and inclination to look at my data and talk to me about it.
- When I am writing the final draft, must be available on e-mail till I complete my dissertation.
- Likely to be doing a proposal within 12 months of starting mine.

Find another student to work with.

When I was doing my dissertation, I didn't quite take an ad out in the campus newspaper (though it may not have been a bad idea!), but I did keep my eyes peeled for people I liked talking to, fellow students I felt comfortable with.

What did I get out of it? Two heads are better than one (a cliché but true). A sounding board. A second pair of eyes that were more readily available than my advisor's. Someone to help me talk my ideas through. She was up at 2:00 A.M. when I had my best ideas. She gave me confidence when my computer crashed and took 25% of the data with it.

What was in it for the shadow researcher? She saw at close

Benefits of working with another student.

1

quarters how a dissertation went and felt more prepared for her turn. In a sense, I was her dress rehearsal! We worked on a paper for one of our classes, based on my data. We collaborated on presentations at conferences based on my data.

Friends are fine, but most of them get quite busy with their own thinking. So go out and get someone you can talk shop to on a regular basis and expect to be understood!

Notes

_____

_____

_____

_____

Contribution 2

Richard Olsen
University of North Carolina at Wilmington

Despite several significant events that happened in my life, I was able to complete my dissertation in one year because of the progress I had made on it during the coursework phase of my study. I was hired ABD [all-but-dissertation] to develop two new courses. My wife was pregnant and delivered our first child in December of that first year teaching. Had it not been for the fact that many of my chapters were at least drafted during coursework projects, I would never have made the deadline my institution set for me.

Using Coursework as Sounding Board

Use coursework as a time to explore the breadth of the discipline and pursue topics, concepts, and research questions that may take only one paper or course to answer. Often this phase is characterized by projects that reflect the interests of the course professor as much as they reflect your own. However, throughout that process you should remain vigilant to note significant topics that might interest you for a dissertation. I kept a file of questions I might want to tackle. Inside the back cover of each course textbook, I wrote research questions (and

Make notes during coursework on possible research topics and questions.

class discussion questions) raised by the book. I kept track of significant questions raised in class discussion as well. This question raising served me well in selecting term projects, and also alleviated the fear that I might not have a good topic for my dissertation.

Using Coursework as Drafting Board

A key to completing the dissertation in a timely manner is being able to draft sections or chapters of the dissertation as you develop term projects for your courses. Ideally, one of your papers will emerge as a particularly intriguing topic that has the depth and significance to expand into a dissertation. Once you have a direction for your dissertation, then other course projects should be grafted onto the dissertation "tree." To do this, it is critical to adapt coursework to the dissertation focus. As you take required courses or electives, the question "How can I advance my dissertation through this course?" should be asked early and often. For instance, for a course on the history of your field, you can do a term paper that explores the historical dimensions of your topic. Everything has a history, so rather than pursuing a generic exercise in historical scholarship, chip away at the literature review. When the mandatory sequence of methods classes presents itself, focus again on the methods section of your dissertation.

Using the Qualifying Exams

The particulars of qualifying exams vary tremendously across graduate programs. Some are "take-home" exams; others are strictly timed events with candidates confined to a room. In either case, there is often a period prior to the exam where candidates meet with professors to discuss possible questions, as well as the interest areas of the student. These conferences are a good time to negotiate a general prompt or even specific question that is tangentially related to the dissertation topic. My own experience was a bit serendipitous. I was given a question on the second day of my qualifying exams that asked me to offer an organizing schema for various approaches to rhetorical criticism. I had not anticipated the question, but the answer actually formed the conceptual basis for the methods chapter in my dissertation.

Each phase of coursework is designed to prepare the student for life after graduation. However, wise use of courses and exam questions can help candidates make significant progress toward completion of the thesis or dissertation even as they complete their coursework.

> Begin writing drafts while taking coursework.

> Adapt coursework to the dissertation focus.

> If possible, request qualifying exam questions related to the dissertation topic.

Notes

_____

_____

_____

_____

Contribution 3

Anonymous
Bemidji, Minnesota

"Writer's block" was common during the early stages of my dissertation, yet I found that I was able to verbally explain a great deal about it. When my advisor or friends would ask me about the topic, or specific questions about the general research question, sample, procedure, literature review, or statistics, I was able to talk at great length, at times even eloquently. I began to carry a tape recorder with me on long road trips when I was alone, and to imagine that an interested and informed passenger was asking about my dissertation. I would record myself providing these explanations, and then transcribe this at a later time into my document. I found it much easier to edit and expand upon this than to simply sit down and write it.

> Use a tape recorder and talk to an imaginary acquaintance.

I also eventually constructed a type of personal behavioral "formula" for my ideal writing conditions. I would exercise heavily during the day so that my body was physically exhausted. I would unplug the phone, get out the popcorn, chips, or peanuts (not so subtly influencing the contrast between my "before" and "after" photos; this would have been deadly without the exercise), and set immediate goals for virtually every paragraph, sometimes a sentence at a time. For example, I wouldn't take a bite until I had finished the next sentence or completed a certain step in the analysis, or would determine that there would be no bathroom break until the next section was done. All such goals had to be established minute by minute, and I became proficient at requiring the optimal amount of progress for the reinforcement available. And, yes, I did gain several pounds in the final tough weeks, when my words-per-peanut ratio was reduced to around 1:1. Amazingly, I still like peanuts.

> Develop a behavioral "formula."

> Hold down the words-to-peanut ratio. **(Ha!)**

4

_____

_____

_____

_____

Contribution 4

Christine L. Ratto
University of Pennsylvania

When faced with the task of writing my dissertation, my immediate thought was, "How am I ever going to write hundreds of pages? This is an enormous amount of work." As a result, I found myself feeling overwhelmed and tended to avoid and procrastinate. I actually found it ironic that my dissertation topic was based on the cognitive model, and I was succumbing to a negative spiral of thoughts, feelings and, consequently, nonproductive behavior! Just noting this pattern was helpful, and in response, I took steps to change my thinking and behavior.

To change my thinking, I was alert to shifts in my mood as I was working on my dissertation. When I experienced a mood shift, I wrote down my thoughts. After about a week, I had collected a full two pages of negative thoughts about the writing process. The prominent themes were, "I am never going to get this done" and a more panicked thought, "What if I can't get this done?" "I went through this whole graduate program for nothing." To counteract these thoughts, I wrote responses that challenged the validity of these cognitions on an index card and left it next to the computer. Then when I noticed a mood shift, I looked at the index card and read the more comforting, and actually, more accurate responses. Examples of responses that challenged my negative thoughts were, "You do not have to get this done today. Just work on this one section. Little by little, you will complete this project" and "You have had these thoughts before about other large tasks in graduate school and have completed them. There is no reason to believe you won't complete this dissertation. You are hard-working and motivated to finish."

Watch out for a negative spiral of thoughts and feelings.

Write down negative thoughts and challenge their validity.

In addition to the steps to change my thinking, I also intervened on a behavioral level. I divided the dissertation into small sections. I would then set monthly, weekly, and daily goals for finishing sections and portions of sections. In doing this, I was able to experience a sense of accomplishment when I finished a small piece, as well as note that I was indeed making progress.

> Divide the dissertation into small sections and set goals.

In sum, I treated myself as a client who needed help counteracting negative feelings that impeded progress on a task. I would suggest that students of psychology not only "talk the talk" but also "walk the walk" and try to use on ourselves some of the techniques we use to motivate people.

> Treat yourself like a client.

Notes

_____

_____

_____

_____

Contribution 5
Anonymous
Adrian, Michigan

One common mistake is to spend too much time writing a first draft for your committee. I labored over this task, hoping to impress the committee with the excellence of my scholarship and prose. Instead, I discovered that each member of my committee had specific desires (I'd call them quirks) for the manuscript and much rewriting was necessary to accommodate their eccentricities. It would have been far better to quickly write a first draft and let the committee members have their say at that time. Don't be worried that they will think your first draft is slipshod; since they didn't write it, they'll think that in any case.

> Avoid trying to write a perfect first draft.

I strongly encourage students not to take a job before completing the dissertation. The demands of a first-year professor are incredible. Adding the task of finishing a dissertation is setting yourself up for a nightmare. If you ignore this advice, then set aside one day a week for

> Complete your dissertation before taking a job.

6

doing nothing but writing.

Having an enforced deadline for completing your degree can be a real motivator. My wife's impending childbirth served that purpose well.

Although smoking is generally a terrible habit, there can be benefits to smoking a pipe during one's orals. Tough questions can be followed by the appropriate slow inhalation, a distant gaze, and the various manipulations that pipe smokers go through. This permits you to look calm while your mind is racing wildly.

Set a series of small goals with rewards for completion of each task. A reward can be as elaborate as a short vacation or as simple as a minor diversion, such as paying bills, watching a little TV, or hitting a punching bag.

A major life event can help you set enforced deadlines.

Try smoking a pipe. (Ha!)

Reward yourself.

Notes

_____

_____

_____

_____

Contribution 6

Jubemi O. Ogisi
Brescia University

Completing a thesis or dissertation has to be seen as a major part of the daunting process of obtaining a graduate degree. The process is more daunting at the doctorate level where many students fail to complete this project.

First of all, many students approach graduate school as an extension of what happened as an undergraduate. Nothing could be furthest from the truth. Graduate students are supposed to be more mature and independent.

As an undergraduate, one accumulates credit hours in order to graduate. On the other hand, graduate school is a process of discrete steps and requirements: completion of courses, candidacy

Recognize the differences between being an undergraduate and being a graduate student.

examination, research proposal, actual research, writing of research, and defending of research. (In some areas like clinical psychology, an approved internship is another part of the process.)

The point is that each of the above-named activities *must* come at various stages of a graduate education. Each step builds on the preceding in a demanding process that culminates in obtaining the graduate degree.

Having said that, let me briefly present a system I used as a graduate student. The system kept me focused: *The student must have a specific goal and a definite plan for achieving this goal.* (Micro-goals, specific plans, and set timetables!)

➢ Step 1: *You must set a specific goal.* Students may assume that because they are enrolled in a Ph.D. program in clinical psychology, this is their goal. NO! It is merely a wish that may never become a reality. This can be changed by…

➢ Step 2: *Set a specific date for achieving your goal.* That is, on the first day of graduate school, you have already set a specific date for completing *all* requirements and obtaining the degree. (Actually, I wrote my goal and plans five years before I returned to graduate school.) The major goal has to have microgoals represented by the steps in the program.

➢ Step 3: *You must write your goal down.* Everything seems important when it is written down. Most important, put your goal where you can see it every day. (I carried mine around on several 3 x 5 index cards. The cards were a daily reminder of what I needed to do to reach my goal.)

➢ Step 4: *You must develop a plan to achieve your goal.* This is where you have to come up with a timetable and specific actions for completing coursework, research proposal, candidacy examination, etc. (I had a timetable that I shared with my advisor. Whenever we met, we both knew what we had to discuss in order to stay on track toward my goal.) Let your advisor advise! You have to come up with a plan!

➢ Step 5: *You must decide the price you are willing to pay.* Completing the entire process of a graduate education takes effort and sacrifice. Certain low-priority items like social, leisure, and recreational activities may have to be curtailed or banished indefinitely. You cannot have it both ways! (While writing my dissertation, I gave my TV to a friend for about six months. You cannot expect to complete your work by watching five or six hours of TV daily.)

A six-step plan for achieving your goal.

Being enrolled in a program is *not* a goal.

Look at your goal every day.

Create a timetable and share it with your advisor.

Curtail or banish low-priority activities.

> Step 6: *You must think about and do something about reaching your goal every day.* This is necessary even at the beginning stages when you have not come up with a research topic. By putting yourself on a regular and habitual routine, it is easier to deal with the inevitable detours that will arise. (When all else fails, read your index cards with your goal.)

Setting a specific goal (with a specific target date) and a definite plan of action will help you measure your progress. Setting a specific goal makes you adequately assess what you really want out of graduate school. Finally, goal setting helps translate a wish into action. However, a goal without a definite plan of action is like obtaining a map of Paris without a plan on how to get there from New York.

Notes

_____

_____

_____

_____

Contribution 7
   Peter Veronesi
   SUNY at Brockport

Chapter II: Review of the Literature...
The Hunter-Gatherers in Us All!

It has been awhile since the majority of humans on this planet have been hunter-gatherers; yet, I feel we must have latent genes for this behavior. This can be seen in those doctoral students who search for elusive descriptors so very necessary for finding "what has been done before you" while you are in the throes of writing your review-of-the-literature chapter.

When doing your lit review, one of your goals (should be) to become familiar with what has been done by other workers in your area of interest. You are becoming the expert in the area of the

---

Do something every day—from the very beginning.

Goal setting helps to translate a wish into action.

knowledge field you are creating. Surprisingly, even more (hopefully) than all those on your committee.

Here's the catch: Since, I believe, we all have a latent gene for hunting and gathering, we can spend our entire lives in a library or at a computer screen amassing volumes of citations without ever reading a single article. In a very short time, you can easily hear yourself saying, "Oh! That's a good one, better tag it!" or "Uuuoooo-eeee! That one fits my idea on...." And so on. And, since you started in January and it is now November, you have obtained over 4 million articles and haven't read a single word! In reality, you should have completed most of your search somewhere from March to May, reading, thinking, and pacing yourself all the while. The point is that once the hunter-gatherer gene kicks in, it is hard to stop. So that you can counter the potential for any latent chromosomal functioning in the area of obtaining resources (in this case articles), I suggest the following:

What to do:

1. Set a specific time that you will say, "*I will be done with 90% of my lit review by _____ and accept those articles I have at this time.*"
2. Read, absorb, synthesize, and write your ideas about what others have described along the way. Your best source of citations comes from the literature reviews of others in an exemplary piece you may be reading. Hopefully, you'll be one of those references some day.
3. Once you have this process complete, go back for no more than a few weeks and complete the rest of your review.

Your committee can point out any shortcomings in your review of the literature at this point. Happy hunting!

Notes

_____

_____

_____

_____

Counter any latent chromosomal functioning.
(Ha!)

Set a definite time for completing 90% of your literature review.

Allow no more than three weeks to complete the rest of the review.

Contribution 8

Aimee L. Franklin
University of Oklahoma

Two things got me through the dissertation process: personal discipline and a strong support network. First, it should be noted that I wrote my dissertation "long distance," (i.e., I was in another state and had to balance this activity with a 30+ hour per week job). In terms of personal discipline, the hardest challenge to overcome was the lack of definite deadlines for the completion of the various components: literature review, prospectus, data gathering, analysis, and write-up. I found that it was easy to let my "self-imposed" deadlines slip since I knew that there were no immediate consequences. To remedy this, I established a very strict policy: Every day, I would spend a minimum of three hours on the dissertation. Some days, this meant I just stared at the computer screen for long periods of time. Other days, this gave me the incentive to get up at 5:00 A.M. and start working, so I could go "play" later in the day. An important benefit of this policy was that I never really fell into the abyss of "writer's block."

The support network consisted mostly of other students in the Ph.D. program. We kept in contact through telephone and e-mail. This aspect of the process was important because you feel very isolated during the dissertation process. This sense of isolation is not surprising since you end up being the world's leading expert on a very narrow topic that is of no real interest to the majority of the world's population. In fact, it may not be all that interesting to your Ph.D. friends, but they can be both a sounding board and a reality check. Just talking out loud about a particularly sticky problem helped me to think it through and come up with solutions. Also, my colleagues served as methodological and analytical police since they had received much of the same scholarly training.

Aim for three hours of work per day with no exceptions.

Feeling a sense of isolation should not be surprising.

Use your Ph.D. friends as a sounding board and reality check.

Notes

_____

_____

_____

_____

Contribution 9

Alec Campbell
Colby College

I used several small tricks to complete my dissertation. First, I had a dissertation group (a set of students at the same point in the process with whom I could share my work). The group included several students working in areas far different than mine. I think it is important to emphasize such a group because while many people recommended that I get involved with one, I resisted for a long time. It was only when I joined the group that I began to make real progress. Second, I think one should seek out the opportunity to give talks based on the completed or even uncompleted parts of the dissertation. I don't necessarily mean only at formal meetings. Talks within the department or even to groups of friends not completing dissertations can be helpful. This helps to think about weaknesses and has the added benefit of preparing for job talks down the road.

As to the writing itself, I had a few small tricks. I always wrote the introductions and conclusions to my chapters after I had completed the body of the text. Since writing is part of the creative process, starting with the introduction makes no sense. The same was true for the introductory and concluding chapters; these were written after the main arguments had been completed. If time is a factor at the end, it pays to make sure that everything is written in the required style as the writing progresses. At my institution, there were myriad rules about margins, footnotes, and spacing. Getting the completed text into the proper format took an entire week. It is a good idea to find the format first and put all but the most trivial text into it at the beginning. Finally, I would recommend keeping track of the bibliography on an ongoing basis. It took me another two days to organize all the citations into a coherent bibliography.

Join a group for real progress.
Talk about your work.
Write introductions and conclusions for chapters after completing the body of the chapters.
Use the required format from the beginning.
Keep track of the bibliography on an ongoing basis.

Notes

_____

_____

_____

_____

Contribution 10

Steve Suter
California State University, Bakersfield

Graduate students in psychology at Johns Hopkins in the late 1960s rigged up the dartboard in the graduate-student lounge so that it became the Dissertation Dartboard. We taped up "Effects of" at the top as the column caption and "On" at the left as the rows caption. Then we added specific labels for individual rows and columns. Each row-by-column intersection yielded a dissertation topic. We made sure that all of our professors' cherished topics were included and generated many opportunities for potentially fruitful collaborations, such as "Effects of Authoritarianism on One-Drop Licking in Rats."

Notes

_____

_____

_____

_____

Create a Dissertation Dartboard. **(Ha!)**

Contribution 11

Anonymous
Little Rock, Arkansas

When undertaking a project of significant size such as a thesis or dissertation, I believe it is helpful to "begin with the end in mind." One useful analogy is of a road map that assists you in getting from Point A (starting) to Point B (completion) and all the steps in-between. As a result, my suggestion to assist students who may be encountering difficulty in the dissertation process involves an educational version of "job-shadowing." In job-shadowing, someone with less knowledge and experience in something observes and interacts closely with someone who has more knowledge and experience in a particular area.

The educational version of this involves identifying another doctoral student who is 2 or 3 "steps" ahead of you in the dissertation

Try job-shadowing a student who is ahead of you.

process, and shadowing them as they complete these tasks. These can include concrete tasks such as how to obtain and complete Human Subjects Review forms, as well as more abstract tasks such as thinking about the most effective ways to present the data from your analyses or writing an abstract that meets your institution's requirements.

Another way to think about this is in terms of a "dissertation buddy system" in which you connect with one other person to de-mystify both the process of writing a dissertation, and all of the sequential steps that must be completed to accomplish the larger task.

In this way, you can "begin with the end in mind," see the completion of the next steps in the immediate future of your dissertation process, and continue to break down the large task of writing a dissertation into smaller steps that can be more easily accomplished in a timely manner.

Begin with the end in mind.

Notes

_____

_____

_____

_____

Contribution 12

Virgil L. Franklin
Virginia State University

I have found that students have a hard time developing the review of literature. I discuss a few helpful ideas with them:

1. Consider developing the review around the variables involved in the study, *or*
2. Consider developing the review as a historical retrospect, *or*
3. Consider reporting the "pros" versus the "cons" and then deciding where the weight of "evidence" seems to fall, *or*
4. Consider reporting or critiquing research procedures, *and*
5. Be sure to conceptualize the entire review with a beginning or introduction, the body or review, and the end or a Johnny Cochran summation.

Possible bases for developing a review of literature.

Other thoughts:

1. Try to stay with literature not more than 10–15 years old.
2. Develop an outline before you finally write.
3. Stay within your hypotheses or research questions.
4. An exhaustive review should entail 20–30 references.

Notes

_____

_____

_____

_____

Contribution 13

Jie Zhang
SUNY College at Buffalo

I have written a master's thesis and a Ph.D. dissertation in two different areas. My master's degree was in linguistics and my Ph.D. in sociology. In the past few years, I have also directed and served on committees for graduate students' theses in the department of sociology. If I were to write another thesis or dissertation, it could be much easier than it was earlier. My suggestions for the students who are working on graduate degrees that require a thesis or dissertation are several as follows.

1. Start to think about the topic of your thesis or dissertation at the very beginning of your graduate program. You may write a term paper on the topic of your interest for one of the beginning courses. Later on for different courses, you may write on the same topic with more information added to it. By the end of your course work, the paper you have developed should be very sophisticated with information from all different courses you have taken that far. This paper could be the draft of your thesis or dissertation.

2. Build literature on your interests from the beginning. If you have two or more focuses you may want to develop your thesis or dissertation with, build different files of literature for each focus.

Consider working on a topic of interest throughout your coursework.

Collect literature from the beginning.

The literature includes not only the citations but also the reprints of the papers. Put the reprinted papers in alphabetical order as they appear in the reference list.

3. Choose the right professor as your advisory committee chair. He or she should be a professor who appears to like you and with whom you feel comfortable. The professor should be one who is willing to spend time with you on your work, and should be one who is highly respected by other faculty in the department. If you happen to choose a professor who does not get along with many others in the department either academically or personally, you are likely to be a victim or scapegoat of their fights.

Don't just collect citations.

For a chair, choose a professor who likes you and is respected by other members of the faculty.

Notes

_____

_____

_____

_____

Contribution 14
Anonymous
Memphis, Tennessee

Choose a tenured faculty member as your main advisor. When I entered the graduate program, I was "gently guided" towards choosing a bright and upcoming junior faculty as my main advisor. When the tenure review came up after three years, this person did not fare well, was turned down, and had to leave the university. I had decided my dissertation topic with this person, conducted my initial literature review, and had even begun working on a dissertation study proposal. As it turned out, the other faculty members were not too keen on my dissertation topic, and so ultimately I had to find a new topic and literally start from scratch. Consequently, *my tenure* as a graduate student was greatly lengthened.

Choose a dissertation topic on which you have some prior knowledge (prior to coming to graduate school, that is). To finish the

Don't lengthen your tenure as a grad student with an untenured advisor.

Prior knowledge of a topic is beneficial.

long trudge of the dissertation process, interest is of course much more important than prior knowledge. But having even a little bit of prior "working knowledge" about the topic facilitates a faster mastery of the topic area. (And mastery of the topic area is, of course, the primary required outcome at the end of the dissertation process.)

Remember you need to pay the rent after you become a Herr Doktor. Living the life of the mind is great, but issues like writing on "hot topics," having the "right" major advisor given the changing academic political climate, and knowing the trends in what types of tenure-track jobs will be offered 4–5 years down the line are becoming increasingly important. Doing a great dissertation is not enough to land a great tenure-track job.

A great dissertation may not be enough to land a great job.

Finally, remember that the faculty are human too (sorry, the movie The Faculty *is wrong!).* The first time I saw my major advisor carrying grocery bags, I was shocked. It was too much of a strain to think of the person as anything else but a scholar. The moral is that students need to learn fast how to productively "handle" the faculty— as they would in any other setting where there is a power differential between "the boss" and them.

See the faculty as human and consider how to handle the power differential.

Notes

_____

_____

_____

_____

Contribution 15
Fred Pyrczak
California State University, Los Angeles

An acquaintance who is a prominent medical sociologist specializing in communications between physicians and patients made a suggestion that also applies to communications between students and committee members. He recommends putting your physical complaints and questions in writing and taking them with you to your

Communicating with committee members.

visit with your physician. With this written material, you won't forget to describe all your symptoms and ask all your questions. In addition, a busy physician will find it hard to rush you out of the office if you have unanswered written questions.

It is important to have written notes on your ideas for thesis or dissertation topics when you first meet with professors to ask them to serve on your committee, especially if you are approaching professors who do not know you well. Undoubtedly, they will ask what your topic or problem area is. If you become flustered and less-than-perfectly articulate, your notes can help you recover. A student who stumbles when answering this basic question may make a poor impression and risk being turned down by the professor.

Write down your ideas for topics before your first meeting, and take your notes with you.

At your first meeting with each potential committee member, you should listen with three purposes. First, is the professor truly interested in your topic or problem area? Second, does the professor have other related topics that you might pursue instead? Keep an open mind on changing the specifics of your topic based on what he or she says. A professor is likely to know what is manageable for a student to undertake as well as which topics and approaches are more likely to yield interesting results. Third, does the professor seem to have enough time to give you the assistance you will need (if you are typical, you will need much assistance)? Does he or she suggest meeting with you on a regular basis? Will you have to wait weeks before you can get another appointment with him or her? Does the professor refer to being extremely busy with his or her commitments to other students and projects? If so, you might consider looking for someone else to be on your committee. On the other hand, there's this saying in the corporate world: "If you want something done, give it to someone who is busy." Thus, you'll have to make a judgment on this question: Is this a busy professor who is efficient and responsive or is this a busy professor who is truly overwhelmed?

Listen with three purposes at your first meeting with potential committee members.

When meeting with your committee members, take careful notes on what they say. First, this will correctly convey that you are a serious student and that you value the help you are receiving. Second, it will save you the embarrassment of having to ask the same questions again because you forgot the original answers. These notes should be carefully stored, preferably in a notebook, for future reference. Keep in mind, however, that your notes do *not* constitute a binding agreement with your professor. Professors are allowed to "think aloud" and change their minds as they get new insights, and you may make errors as you take notes. However, written notes will reduce the potential for confusion and miscommunication.

Take notes on what your committee members say when you meet with them.

Your notes are not a binding contract.

18

Notes

_____

_____

_____

_____

Contribution 16

Michel Caconis
Grand Valley State University

1. The student should prioritize her/his interests in and about research. Is prompt graduation critical? Is a particular type of research project a consideration? Are funding, type, and duration considerations influencing other decisions? Are relationships with advisor and committee considerations? Is there work going on in the department in which you might participate? Is there a project going on at your job that might make a decent research topic? Do you wish to make a large splash in your field? Are you using the conduct of this project to open other doors? Do you have an opportunity or need for funding that will influence your project? Is there something you just love or really want to know which can serve as a motivation for follow-through?

   Questions for self-reflection.

2. The student should read other theses from his/her department, a related field, or from a similar program if no other option is available.

   Read the theses written by others.

3. If stuck for ideas, check past years of journals and look at research recommendations in articles and research abstracts. Also, check newsletters of organizations for themes. Free-write about ideas. Concept-map about ideas generated in free-writing.

   Suggestions for getting ideas for topics.

4. If still stuck for ideas, review Dissertation Abstracts and, of course, talk with others at school, in the field, in organizations where you have a relationship or interest and ask for needed research.

5. Plan for your project activities to take a bit more time than you think when you do an initial timeline for your project completion.

   Plan on it taking more time.

6. Let computers help you. Gain familiarity with programs that can help you organize even your literature review. Borrow a laptop to take to the library and to do your "note cards" on computer files, which you can later "cut-and-paste" for your proposal/thesis.

7. Partialize activities. Don't think: *thesis* and *thesis defense*. Think: questions, writing a paragraph/chapter; editing these 10 pages; lit review in a particular library; check the WWW for information; make a phone call to a friend; go to a movie; input 10 cases in next hour; transcribe interviews for two hours then take a walk; etc. Do manageable bits, being realistic in timeframe development. Think of your work habits and your strengths and limitations and work with and around and through them.

8. Listen to relaxation tapes, do yoga, exercise, and the like. (I do this now to reduce anxiety and sense of being overwhelmed. However, I ate chocolate, smoked, and drank diet soda when writing my dissertation: *not* good as I'm paying for that now. Fun then, not fun now.)

9. Have reliable editors available to read your very rough, rough, and final drafts.

10. Get *clear* about department and university guidelines for the writing, organization, timelines, due dates, etc. the *sooner the better*. Check with officials, then with colleagues, then with officials again. Officials usually win these debates.

11. *Build in time for what you think is fun*—as a reward, as a means to maintaining social contact and continuing relationships, and to help you generate down-time, which further generates thinking for your research.

Notes

_____

_____

_____

_____

Make note cards using a laptop.

Don't think "*thesis defense.*"

Think in terms of the pieces.

Fun then, not fun now.

Use reliable editors.

Double-check the guidelines/rules with officials.

Reward yourself.

Contribution 17
Debra Harvey Swanson
Hope College

I was the kind of student that Becker describes in *Writing for Social Scientists: How to Start and Finish Your Thesis, Book or Article*—the kind of student who first cleaned the house, then organized all of my writing utensils, books, and snacks before I could begin writing. Sometimes that would use up two hours of my writing time. No wonder I was so frustrated at how slowly the process seemed to be going. My advisor, Dr. John McCarthy, gave me some very simple advice, but it worked. Use your writing time to Write! If during this time you can't think anymore, work on the bibliography or make the tables/graphics, but do something. Don't allow other things to use up your writing time. In a sense, Becker says the same thing with his idea about a "spew draft"; put something down on paper because it will be easier to revise than it will be to write the perfect first draft. Now doesn't that seem logical? Yet, I wasn't doing it until after our little talk.

> Use your writing time to *Write!*

> Try writing a "spew draft."

The other thing I learned while doing my dissertation was that dissertation writing is not like other writing. With most writing, you try to be innovative, creative, and precise. The dissertation is very pedantic. The formula for each chapter is: "This is what I am going to say in this chapter, this is what I am saying, this is what I have just said," repeating it for each chapter. This allows outside readers to read just one chapter before your defense and to act like they understand the whole; they do not want to have to read/skim the whole thing—no matter how brilliant it may be.

> A three-part "formula" for each chapter.

After all of this writing and agonizing, the defense is somewhat anticlimactic. While my defense was not stellar, I actually enjoyed talking to informed folks about the data and my findings. And, while I was sweating, in the long run it didn't seem like the discussion was long enough for all the time and work I put into the manuscript. My advice, then, is don't forget to celebrate the finish. It is important even if you are caught up in the busyness of other academic duties or job-hunting. You are done! (Moms like to receive copies of your dissertation for their coffee tables, but other family members will just smile and look for their names in the acknowledgments.)

> The defense can be anticlimactic.

> Be sure to celebrate.

> Don't forget mom's coffee-table copy. (**Ha!**)

Notes

_____

_____

_____

_____

Contribution 18

Carol B. Furtwengler
Wichita State University

We try to keep our students on a tight schedule to have their dissertations completed on time. Some of these suggestions apply to things students can do; others apply to things faculty can do (included below as parenthetical material).

Tips for finishing your dissertation on time:

- Have your proposal completed during the last semester that you are enrolled in content coursework. Once you leave campus and the security found in fellow students and faculty, it is too easy to have your time and commitment redirected toward job and family responsibilities. Leaving campus with a blueprint under your arm allows you to begin the dissertation process without missing a beat.

  Don't leave campus without an approved proposal.

- Once your proposal is completed and approved, immediately complete your institution's forms for human rights protection for research. (Our department gives the forms to students as soon as the proposal is approved and has students complete the forms before leaving that day.)

  Submit a human rights protection form as soon as possible.

- Meet with colleagues once a week for breakfast during the time you are working on your dissertation. (Our department has a cohort program, and students meet to discuss their problems and progress and to receive support from one another. Faculty often join these early morning breakfast sessions.)

  Meet with colleagues regularly.

- Be sure you have everything you need from your institution before you leave campus. Do you need letterhead for consent forms?

Help with your form for approval of your research? Is your program of study signed and sent to the graduate school?

- Ask your department to develop a template for a dissertation or find a student who loves technology and have one created. (We keep a dissertation template on our department's server for students to use. It has all the requirements of the graduate school built into the formatting. Section breaks separate chapters with correct pagination and with directions for what usually belongs in each chapter. We also keep university stationery letterhead for consent forms on the server for students to download.)

- Buy EndNote 3.0 software from Niles Associates and keep all of your literature review information in an electronic file. This wonderful program allows you to search by key words, and you can enter your notes by major topics within your dissertation. You can print out just the sections that pertain to that topic and use these notes as you write. EndNote also allows you to insert citations and automatically does your reference list in the style sheet that you select.

> Try to get a template for use while writing.

> Computerize your citations and references.

Notes

_____

_____

_____

_____

Contribution 19

Dean McGovern

The University of Montana

My suggestion has only to do with the writing portion of the thesis/dissertation process. I did not struggle as much with the conceptualization and data collection aspects of my master's thesis. It was the data analysis and writing process that had me tied in knots.

Easily one of the most important things I learned while struggling through my master's thesis was *how* I work. I found it enlightening and, in a sense, liberating to discover how I work best. Writing time, distractions, environment, workstations, snacks, exercise patterns all emerged as important to my work process. As I suspect is the case with most folks, I didn't pay attention to these things at first. Rather, I worried about time fleeting and deadlines passing and watched day after day go by without much in the way of product—that is, until I discovered my pattern.

I'm somebody who needs to work hard for a while and then put the project aside for a bit of time. In my case, I didn't look at my project for a week. When I'd return to it, it appeared differently, and with fresh eyes, I could more clearly see where the project needed attention. Also, with my head down and constantly working hard, I would lose perspective, purpose, and eventually desire. I found that if I took periodic "breaks" from the project, I was often eager to return to it and was much more productive.

Notes

_____

_____

_____

_____

Contribution 20

Gary Helfand
University of Hawaii, West Oahu

Try to cultivate an interest from one or more of the courses you have completed prior to beginning the thesis or dissertation. Think about all of the term papers you've written and decide whether one of these could ultimately be expanded into a thesis or dissertation topic. When teaching at the graduate level, I encourage students to think about their thesis continuously as they go through the program. I inform them that, from my own experience of over 25 years of teaching and advising students, those who frequently have the greatest

> Discover *how* you work best.

> Consider putting the project aside for a while and coming back with fresh eyes.

difficulty getting through the thesis or dissertation are individuals who come to the thesis seminar the first day without a clue regarding a topic. Second, once a student develops a real interest in a topic (usually when he/she is somewhere in the middle of their coursework), the next crucial element is to narrow the scope so that collection of primary data is feasible. Once the research topic has been narrowed and clearly defined, the student needs to decide what kind of research *method(s)* would be most appropriate for the collection of data. Usually, this means that a course in research methodology needs to be completed early in the graduate program so that a student becomes familiar with when and how to use various methods such as surveys, field studies, experiments, content analyses, focus groups, etc. While statistics courses are often seen as abstract and of questionable value for the future careers of many students, a basic understanding of quantitative techniques is needed in order for the student to successfully finish the data analysis chapter, which always appears near the end of a thesis or dissertation.

Finally, one other recommendation: When a student seems to be overwhelmed by the sheer size, depth, and/or comprehensiveness of a thesis and especially a dissertation, I always suggest that they think of it as a series of closely connected or integrated term papers. Since they have already completed numerous term papers, they usually realize that they do, in fact, have the capacity to complete the thesis or dissertation.

Notes

_____

_____

_____

_____

| Bring ideas with you the first day of a thesis seminar. |
| Take research methods classes early. |
| Think of the dissertation as a series of integrated term papers. |

Contribution 21

Lisa Ann Hollis-Sawyer
Northeastern Illinois University

In my experiences at both ends of the spectrum (graduate student and thesis advisor), I have developed a certain strategy when approaching such a task. I think the most important fact to realize, whether a student or advisor, is that the task appears to be rather overwhelming. To address this reaction, I advise my students to follow the tenets of Goal Setting Theory. Specifically, break down the goal of doing a thesis and/or dissertation into manageable subgoals (e.g., complete literature review) and set deadlines that are reasonable but stringently paced.

Why set "goals" in such a manner when doing a thesis or dissertation? One of the main reasons derives itself from the self-efficacy literature. One is more likely to successfully "master" a broad-based goal if the task goal is divided into several subgoals that are easily achievable in a successive manner over time, and repeated past experiences of mastery help in further goal-setting behavior. Further, from the cognitive psychology literature, to set reasonable but progressively paced goals helps the student to narrow his/her focus and devote his/her cognitive resources to a small task, optimizing the level of task proficiency. A person is limited in attentional resources, to varying degrees in different contexts, and the dividing of a large task goal (i.e., completing a thesis or dissertation) into subgoals helps address these resource capacity limitations, as well as helps reduce anxiety which also potentially affects level of attentional resources in task performance. Last, but not least, the advisor has the role of being a facilitator in this process, helping the student meet the goals with corrective, positive feedback.

> Consider Goal Setting Theory.

> Using subgoals helps reduce anxiety.

Notes

_____

_____

_____

_____

Contribution 22

Michael Slater
Colorado State University

Here are some guidelines for proceeding through the thesis or dissertation process. These are not definitive; every thesis, every committee has its own idiosyncrasies. The advice and preferences of your advisor and committee members always take precedence. Nonetheless, these suggestions may prove helpful. And remember what an advisor of mine told me: "This dissertation may or may not be your first piece of research; hopefully, it won't be your last piece of research; and almost certainly, it won't be your best research. So just get it done!"

1. Develop a timetable for completing your thesis or dissertation with your advisor's help. Work backward from when you want to graduate. You may well find that you are already behind before you begin. Review the departmental grad manual and the grad school manual for additional guidelines and policies.

2. Never schedule a proposal meeting or defense until you have had all committee members respond to a draft proposal or thesis/project and you've determined as best you can that no members have serious problems with any aspect of your draft; this will prevent many nasty surprises. And never circulate anything to your other committee members until your advisor has seen it and given a go-ahead.

3. Make sure you allow at least several weeks for committee members to read and respond to your draft, and then you may or may not need additional time to do significant revisions for one or more committee members. Make sure that each is reasonably satisfied before formally meeting. Get the department form signed after the proposal meeting by all committee members, which provides formal assent to the scope of your proposal.

4. Get your human subjects form in process as soon as possible after the proposal meeting. It needs to be submitted in the department as well as to the university, and the university committee meets only once a month and has a deadline—check to confirm the correct date. You will need to have a completed draft of your questionnaire instrument, sample stimuli, etc.

5. Make sure you circulate your draft questionnaire, stimuli, procedures, and planned data analysis strategy to your committee members for comment before going ahead and collecting data.

6. As you analyze your results, circulate a description of analyses/results to your committee, asking for comments and suggestions (better now than later during write-up when you don't want to be doing more analyses, though you may still wind up

---

Your dissertation almost certainly won't be your best research.

Establish a timetable.

Circulate a draft proposal before scheduling a proposal meeting or defense.

Never circulate anything without your advisor's approval.

The Human Rights Committee might meet only once a month. Submit the form as soon as possible.

Get approval on methods before collecting data.

doing some).

7. If you have data analysis problems, see your advisor/committee members first (if it is just a problem with a program that won't run, first see if any of your grad student colleagues can spot the problem). Go for outside help at your advisor's recommendation only. If you need to speak to a faculty member in this or another department who is not on your committee, call and make an appointment, after clearing it with your advisor.

8. Find out from each committee member if he/she would prefer to read each chapter as it is drafted, or read the whole manuscript at one time. Also, find out how much lead time each member expects to get back to you on your drafts, and honor that lead time.

9. Get the whole manuscript, when completed, to each committee member (*after* your advisor has looked at it and said it is ready to circulate). Provide some sort of time frame, e.g., "I'm hoping to defend in about six weeks if there are no major problems with the draft—I'd appreciate it if you could get back to me in two weeks [or whatever their preferred lead time is] so I can make sure to make necessary revisions in time." Even if members have read individual chapters, be prepared for additional changes and additional analyses. It takes time for committee members to really understand and think clearly about what you are doing. This is also a good time to get your draft to the graduate office to make sure that you are meeting your format requirements for the thesis, if you are doing a thesis; fixing problems now will save headaches later. If there are any significant problems after the draft reading, don't schedule the proposal meeting or defense until they have been resolved.

10. Get the revised manuscript to your committee members at least 10 days–two weeks [longer, if they express that preference] before the defense date. Have it in final form; if you are lucky, you may walk out of the defense ready to just hand it in! This may mean a lot of annoying trips back and forth to the graduate office to make sure it is done right.

11. Prepare a 15–20 minute summary of your research for your defense, with overheads and handouts. Practice it. Talk to your advisor about the defense and what to expect.

12. After the defense, get your form signed by the committee members and get the form to the graduate dean's office right away. So bring that form to the defense, along with the signature pages in proper format, on approved acid-free paper! (The pages might not get signed at the defense; your adviser may hold them until changes are made. Often, though, other committee members may sign off then to save time if changes are minor.)

13. Make sure you are clear on any final needed changes in discussion with your advisor. Submit those changes to your advisor with the

Do committee members want to read each chapter as it is drafted? How much lead time does each one want?

Be prepared to make additional revisions.

Have it in final form for the defense.

Prepare for the defense. Learn what to expect.

signature pages; get those circulated and your thesis into the graduate office.

14. Give a bound copy of the thesis to the department, in addition to the other copies required by the grad school.

Notes

_____

_____

_____

_____

Contribution 23
Marla Berg-Weger
St. Louis University

Thoughts on the doctoral process:

- Identify your area of study/research early in your doctoral training. This allows you to begin to build your literature base, and you can build assignments, projects, papers and research assistantships around your area of interest.

- Annotate *everything!* Have a form and format for annotating and maintaining literature. You can use either a manual or computer-based literature management system, but organization is the key.

- Get to know the faculty early on even if you do not have them for instructors in your classes. They are potential committee members/chair, mentors, co-authors, references, or "employers" (i.e., can hire you to work on a grant they have received).

- Get and stay involved in school, university, community, and/or professional activities. These are excellent opportunities for networking, data collection resources, collaboration, and identifying potential committee members and current or future employers/colleagues. Being involved enables you to become/stay current on the issues in your area of interest, academic life. Check to see if you can serve as an academic advisor or internship liaison or serve on a school/university committee. This is a great

Annotate everything.
Be organized.

Get involved in other academic activities.

experience to prepare you for academic life.

- When identifying and defining your area of research for your thesis or dissertation, keep it simple! Remember, the dissertation is *not* your life's work. Your goal is to complete the dissertation or thesis to fulfill the requirements for graduation so that you can go forward and actually do your life's work!

- Plan on the process taking longer than your original schedule targeted.

- Make certain that your committee members are not planning a sabbatical the semester in which you plan to defend your dissertation or thesis. If the committee member is planning to be away from the campus, determine your options (i.e., can you retain that person on your committee or must you locate a replacement committee member?).

- As you are completing the writing phase of your dissertation or thesis and you are meeting with your committee members, obtain "closure" at the end of each of these sessions. Specifically, discuss with the faculty member the scheduling of your next meeting with him/her, expectations of you and the faculty member in the interim, deadlines, etc.

- Stay flexible and open—do not become wedded to your words and ideas to the point of immobilization. You want to avoid a "standoff" with your chair or committee members because you refuse to incorporate their recommendations. If you opt not to incorporate faculty suggestions and recommendations into your work, have a logical and well-articulated rationale.

- Learning does *not* have to be painful! Try not to take on a defensive or adversarial stance with the chair or faculty members of your committee. In the end, they *will* persevere!

- Do not neglect other areas of your professional or personal life during the dissertation/thesis phase. Balance is best!

- Do not allow setbacks (i.e., rewriting, conducting additional analyses, gathering more literature, etc.) to immobilize you—keep plugging away at the process!

- If you should become immobilized for internal or external reasons, ask for help from an appropriate resource. Such a resource may be a faculty member, colleague, or mental health professional.

- Expect the dissertation or thesis process to resemble a roller coaster, particularly regarding your emotions. Research, in ideal situations, includes peaks and valleys and feasts and famines, but is particularly "fluid" during the dissertation or thesis process.

- During the down times (i.e., your committee is reading the latest

Your dissertation is *not* your life's work.
Plan on the process taking longer than you anticipated.
Seek closure at the end of each meeting with committee members.
Avoid a standoff with your committee.
Seek help if you become immobilized.
Don't be surprised if it's like a roller coaster.
Use your "down time" wisely.

draft, and you are awaiting their feedback), make good use of your time. You can work on annotating more literature, prepare for the next step in the process (e.g., orals, defense, etc.), refine your curriculum vitae, begin the employment search process, and/or edit your work.

- Anticipate the process, particularly the defense of your dissertation/thesis. Your anxiety may be reduced by attending other students' defenses, talking with others who have successfully completed the process, forming a student support group, rehearsing your defense with your chair, etc. Information is power!

- Be committed to and vigilant about self-care—physical and mental health. Getting a graduate degree should not control your life!

- Perseverance! Just keep plugging away unless you feel you have lost your passion about your work. Should this occur, consider taking a break or changing your area of focus. Both of these are risks, however, that you feel you may not be able to take at this point.

- Resist the temptation to personalize the feedback that you receive from faculty members regarding your ideas, writing, etc. Have a trusted person that you can "reality check" with on a regular basis.

- Establish a specific, measurable, achievable plan for accomplishing the seemingly overwhelming task of completing a dissertation or thesis. Having a plan in place compartmentalizes the cumbersome process into achievable parts in which you can be successful. Success breeds success!

- If you are planning a career in academia, try to write for publication during your graduate experience. Publications lead to jobs!

Notes

_____

_____

_____

_____

Attend other students' defenses.

Information is power.

Perseverance!

Don't personalize feedback from faculty.

Contribution 24

Steve Barney
Southern Utah University

   Upon taking the extended-year plan to finish my dissertation, I have amassed several tricks or techniques that would certainly have been of benefit to me had I chosen to use them.

   Choosing a topic: Select a topic that is of some personal interest. You will be inundated with this topic within the first few months. If it is something you really like and have some personal connection with, the task will become barely manageable rather than intolerable. Once a topic is selected, eliminate any delusions you may have for making a significant contribution to science or to your school of thought. Unless you are among the very brightest students, these grandiose ideas are a sure way to put yourself on the 10-year plan. Think of the simplest, cleanest, and quickest project your committee will accept—then do it. If things turn out, your results may be sufficient for publication, or they may not. I know of no jobs given to non-degreed individuals just because they were working on a groundbreaking thesis or dissertation project. Get the initials behind your name, then strive for publication, if that is your calling.

   Writing a literature review: Get to know the people at the reference desk on a first-name basis. If they like you and know what you happen to be looking for, it is possible that they may take the time to let you know when a much-needed book has been returned or a current issue of a journal comes in. Also, if your library is as incomplete as the ones I used, the interlibrary loan office should be a second home of sorts. I found that gifts of chocolate chip cookies or donuts to the right people in the library expedited several aspects of my literature review.

   Read at least one article or chapter in a relevant area every other day. If the article is something you may be using, take a few notes on a separate page and staple the page to the top of the article (only if you have your own personal copy. The above-mentioned individuals at the library will not appreciate stapling paper to their bound journals. Even donuts will not compensate for this type of behavior). Also, get into the habit of typing an APA-style reference for each article you consider using in your project. This sure saves a lot of time and effort toward the end of the process.

   Writing: The first trick is simply to write. Write at least one page per day, even if what you write is garbage, and for me it usually was. The next day, before writing your page for that day, read anew what

Grandiose ideas can put you on a 10-year plan to graduation.

Get to know people at the reference desk.

Donuts may help.

Read one article every other day.

But donuts won't always work. **(Ha!)**

The first trick is to write—write anything.

you had written. I found that I usually kept about three or four good sentences on average from the previous day's work.

I found myself becoming so absorbed by my dissertation that I knew everything about it—every word, every comma, every capital letter—even when they did not exist or were somehow transported to the wrong place. I became so narrow-sighted I could not read what I had written objectively anymore. At this stage, I found it incredibly helpful for someone who knew nothing about my topic to read my document and try to follow what I was doing and how I was expressing myself. Those with captive audiences such as spouses or adult children who can be "guilted" into doing this for you are extremely fortunate. Those of you without such resources—be prepared to pay big favor points at some time in the future. Regardless, this is a worthwhile price to pay.

Finally: When you think you have a pretty good idea of what you are doing, and your objective reader has some clue what you are trying to accomplish, send a draft to your advisor or to another committee member for feedback. It certainly helps to get them involved in the process early. The benefits of feedback from these sources early in your project can prove fruitful in the future, like on Defense Day.

> Get someone who knows nothing about your topic to give you feedback.

> Get feedback early.

Notes

_____

_____

_____

_____

Contribution 25

Dan Johnson
University of North Carolina, Wilmington

The most efficient piece of advice I received that helped me finish my Ph.D. was given to me by a colleague when I was an instructor at a university. She implored me to decide on a research topic as soon as

> Select a topic as soon as possible.

possible. She argued that the sooner I chose a topic the sooner I could begin reading and that I could then focus as many papers as possible in school on that topic, essentially killing two birds with one stone.

I started a file of ideas for a topic, adding to the list periodically when a topic sounded interesting. Not surprisingly, I ended up choosing the first topic I wrote down, but the process allowed me to finalize the choice rather than choose one by default.

Furthermore, picking my topic early allowed me to do focused reading for two years before starting school again. I was able to see the big picture of the topic longer before narrowing the research. I also was able to look at different possibilities, later incorporating my research into a paid job.

Because I had completed preliminary reading, I was able to start writing papers on my topic the first semester of my program. Two independent studies, multiple papers later, and a focused topic as a guide in my research classes left me with a publication, multiple national presentations, and a large literature review long before putting my proposal together. Many of my fellow students waited until they had completed their class work before choosing a topic, essentially starting a new process that would extend their stay at the university.

Notes

_____

_____

_____

_____

Waiting to select a topic can extend your stay at the university.

Contribution 26
Pamela Schuetze
Buffalo State College

Based on my own experiences completing my dissertation in developmental psychology, I have several suggestions that may ease this long and, at times, arduous process for you. Perhaps the most important decisions you will make to ensure that this process runs as smoothly as possible are selecting and designing your project and selecting the committee members that will be available to you for advice, instruction, and, ultimately, evaluation. The project you select for your dissertation should, ideally, be a large enough project to result in one or more publications but should not be so unwieldy that you are unable to finish it within a reasonable amount of time. Care should also be taken to select a study that you are fairly certain will yield publishable findings. The best person to help you select and modify your topic is your advisor. However, if you are not certain that the adviser is conscientious in working with you to select an appropriate and manageable project, do not be hesitant to bounce your ideas off other professionals or experts in the field as well as your fellow students. Conferences are great opportunities to meet and talk with other professionals who are interested in the same fields of study as yourself. Take advantage of these opportunities. If such opportunities are not available to you, create them by e-mailing or calling these individuals. In most cases, professionals are more than happy to discuss their own work and share their expertise with you.

Selecting a committee for your dissertation defense is another important decision that is often overlooked by students. Although it is unarguably important to select individuals who will be able to contribute knowledge and advice to your specific topic, consideration must also be made to the personalities of the individuals. In other words, take care not to select committee members who will have considerable trouble working together. It is not unusual to hear of students who had difficulty completing their requirements because committee members were unable to agree on various aspects of the project or because they refused or were unable to work together efficiently. Talk to other students to find out who these individuals are and use this information to make your decision about your committee.

If these initial decisions are made carefully, you have set a solid foundation for the project. This, unfortunately, does not ensure smooth sailing. Expect problems to crop up. Research rarely runs smoothly without any hitches. When setting your own personal deadlines to complete the project, allow "wiggle" room. This will protect you from undue frustration. Having said that, I do recommend that you break your project down into a series of subgoals and that you set tentative deadlines that you personally would like to reach. Make sure that they are realistic deadlines and then work diligently to reach these goals. For example, as you collect your data, manage it and enter it into your statistical software package file instead of saving piles of data for the

Select a project that is publishable but not unwieldy.

Select a committee that can work well together.

Allow "wiggle" room in setting your deadlines.

end of your data collection process. Not only does this save you from very long and tedious data entry sessions, but it also reduces the likelihood that you will make errors during the data entry process because you are working under a much more manageable schedule. Many students fall into the trap of procrastination and three, four, or even five years later still find themselves trying to complete their dissertation. While the life of a student *can* be fun, it is nice to use that degree for which you have been working so hard. Good luck, it's worth it in the end.

The life of a student *can* be fun, but….

Notes

_____

_____

_____

_____

Contribution 27

Barbara Keating
Minnesota State University, Mankato

One mistake graduate students often make is to wait for a block of time to tackle this big project. But it is a rare person that can actually get an entire morning or afternoon free from commitments or interruptions much less the weeks and months a thesis takes.

Don't wait until you can find a big block of time.

Another student in my Ph.D. program (1970s) got her dissertation done more efficiently than the rest of us. Instead of waiting for a block of free time, she made a two-hour appointment with herself on her calendar every day. To my knowledge, she kept that appointment by giving it high priority and did not break the appointment with herself. She worked on her thesis for two hours every day but only two hours, so she kept up with other commitments also.

Consider using two hours a day—but only two hours.

I finally did something similar when I started as an assistant professor here at Mankato State in 1981 with my dissertation unfinished. My family stayed in Nebraska that first year, so I was commuting to Nebraska every other weekend. While in Mankato, I worked in my campus office all day on my teaching work but did not take teaching work home to my small apartment. I worked on my dissertation for two or three hours almost every evening. Even with new teaching preparations and commuting 300 miles each way on alternate weekends, I made steady progress on my dissertation and finished it during my first quarter.

Notes

_____

_____

_____

_____

Contribution 28

Janis Johnston
University of Wyoming

Many people enter graduate programs only to finish the coursework and never finish their dissertations or thesis. Among the potential problems are not having a clear idea about the thesis/dissertation topic and leaving the school environment early.

The first rule to completing a dissertation or thesis is to choose a topic that you are absolutely passionate about. Too many people select a topic based on how easy it will be to compile data or how quickly they can "get it over with." Ostensibly, people at this level are already in a discipline that has their interest. Don't ruin that by choosing a paper topic that is boring.

Implicit in this idea is that you know what you want to write about and have it started before your last semester of school starts. It is very easy to put the thesis or dissertation off early in your classwork, but if you lay some of the preliminary groundwork during the first couple of semesters, it will give you the time to work on something you want to do rather than something you have to do.

It also helps if one does not consider the thesis or dissertation as though it was a single entity, but rather think of working on the

> Consider your passions when selecting a topic.

separate chapters as though they were individual papers. This technique is great for the rough draft and is less foreboding than thinking of the thesis or dissertation as one large document. You can work on the segues between chapters after the main ideas for each chapter are done, and even include small chapters to connect main points. Breaking it into smaller pieces makes it a more manageable project.

My final suggestion would be to finish the paper before you leave school. Many people have left school without having finished their thesis, fully intending to have it done during the next couple of months, then defend and graduate. The demands of the "real world" can pull you away from this task, however, and it is easy to put it on the back burner, thinking, "I can work on this next week." The longer the project is put off, the harder it is to get back to until so much time has passed it seems pointless to even try.

There are many reasons to finish your degree, not the least of which is the personal satisfaction of completing something that is important to you. These points worked for me; I hope they can help someone else.

Notes

_____

_____

_____

_____

Contribution 29
Brian Fry
Southern Nazarene University

1. For each article or book I read, I typed up notes (containing verbatim quotes, personal commentaries, and connections with other readings). On the tab of each folder, I wrote the name of the author (or first author), the year of publication, and title. When it came time to summarize a body of research, or to compare my findings with the

---

Think of the chapters as individual papers.

Finish before you leave school.

Type and file notes on what you read.

literature, I rarely opened a book. I simply opened my file drawer, pulled out the relevant folders, reviewed them, and began to write. I am convinced that this saved me hundreds of hours during the writing phase of the dissertation. The investment is up front, but the dividends pay for themselves in short order. In fact, a year after completing the dissertation, I am still using my files for other research articles and lectures. The file system also provided me with hope—I had tangible notes of what I read, and my ability to recall facts and figures improved dramatically.

2. I also kept a timeline of self-imposed deadlines on a master calendar. I was very specific. For example, I would indicate that section one of chapter six would be completed by June 21. I would treat the deadline as if it were a real deadline—one imposed by my advisor or another committee member. I sometimes stayed up all night to meet these self-imposed deadlines. The "trick" is to consider them nonnegotiable.

The files can be useful even after completing the dissertation.

Create a master calendar.

Notes

_____

_____

_____

_____

Contribution 30
Kelly Damphousse
University of Oklahoma

Get started. Break your dissertation up into small, easily digested chunks. The key is the *outline*. Start with a basic outline: Introduction, Problem Statement, Theory/Literature Review, Hypotheses, Data, Methods, Results, Conclusion, and References. Put a page break between each new section. Wow! In five minutes, you will have "written" the first nine pages of your dissertation. Once you've done this, write a summary paragraph for each section. Don't concentrate too much on details or citations at this stage. In general terms, just

Start with a basic outline.

Write a summary paragraph for each section.

write down what you think each section will say. This will help in the next step, where you create a more detailed outline for each of the sections. You may be drawing upon three different literatures, or you may be using two different data sets. Give each topic a subsection heading, and then write a short summary paragraph for each. Once the detailed outline is complete, go back and write a polished opening paragraph for each major section. This will help give coherence to the chapter as you return to write in it later. Describe the subsections that will follow and how they fit into the scheme of your dissertation. Now you are ready to really start writing. When you have time, pick a section and start writing in it. During a week that you really feel energized, knock out that long subsection. When you feel less energized, write a paragraph describing your data, create some tables for the results section, or catch up on your citations.

Give subsections headings and write a paragraph for each.

Select each writing task based on your energy level.

Notes

_____

_____

_____

_____

Contribution 31
Herbert W. Helm, Jr.
Andrews University

A Time Orientation to Your Dissertation

While working on my dissertation I was also doing a full-time internship, so time was a precious commodity. One of the techniques to help finish my dissertation was a "time-oriented" approach. This "time-oriented" philosophy stated that I had to put in a certain amount of time in a given week (there were minimal exceptions). This time was put in no matter how much got accomplished during that time period, and I was to work consistently during that time. In order to feel that you can do this, a reasonable amount of time needs to be chosen. For example, I believe that I had to put in three days (it is best

Develop a time orientation.

to specify which days) in a given week with a minimum of two hours each day. Of course, one can always put in more, but this is a minimum. If you get a lot done during this time, that's great. If you only rework a small portion, that is also acceptable. You are successful if you keep working for the whole time period. My worst night was when I looked for a piece of paper for the whole time. It was frustrating. I decided to take my next time period and organize my materials better. This helped on future nights also. However, it was still successful (though frustrating) because the "time orientation" was kept. In the long run, that session was a step toward the final goal. During this "time-oriented" approach, you will probably discover a couple of concepts. First, there will be times that you may want or choose to work more than the minimum. There may be times you get excited about some aspect you are working on, you may have a deadline, or you may need to take a day here and there to do things like data collection and analysis. Second, by doing a little bit at a time, it does add up. This is especially true if you incorporate this concept with larger time blocks. The bottom line is that by picking a minimal time period on a reasonable number of days, you should be able to convince yourself to work toward the completion of your project, and over time, it will occur.

Notes

_____

_____

_____

_____

Use a time period to get organized.

Select a minimum amount of time, but you may want to extend it.

Contribution 32

George Denny
University of Arkansas

Rule of 19:

To make sure in APA style that all references are cited and all citations are referenced:

1. Open the complete paper on the word processor, and print the reference list.
2. From the top of the paper, have the word processor search for the string "19." It will stop for every citation from 1900 to 1999.
3a When a citation is not on the reference list, add its reference.
3b When a citation is on the reference list, put a checkmark by it.
3c When a citation involving 3 to 5 authors already has a checkmark by it on the reference list, change the citation to "et al." as in APA style.
4. Remove any unchecked references from the reference list.

This rule suffers from the Y2K problem, so after 2000 it becomes the Rule of 19 & 20, and Step 2 will need to be done twice, once for "19" and once for "20."

Master Bibliography:

Whenever you first get a reference you may use, add it in correct APA style to a word processor file that is your Master Bibliography. Annotate if desired. Whenever the reference is used in a paper, a copy-and-paste can transfer the reference from the bibliography to the paper. For many people, the dissertation process is a good time to start their Master Bibliography. Back up this file often!

Find a quiet place that is free of distractions to write:

When writing my dissertation, I got permission from my church to use one of their Sunday School classrooms during the week. I would set up my computer and materials on Monday and leave them set up until Friday or Saturday. The church had fewer distractions and interruptions than home, work, or the library.

Keep a to-do list handy during a writing session:

All sorts of things will come to mind that need to be done when it is time to write. Jot them down on a list so you do not forget them later, but get back to your writing now.

Use the "Rule of 19" to make sure all citations are referenced.

Create a Master Bibliography.

Consider using a church setting!

Keep a to-do list.

Use lots of headings and subheadings as you write:

During the writing process, they can be used as place holders—indicating topics you plan to address later as you move ahead to write on other topics. For the reader, they help signal transitions and shifts of focus. A rule of thumb: Average one heading or subheading per double-spaced page.

Use of first person (I, me, my) in writing:

Be sure to find out early on from your committee whether they allow or encourage use of the first person in your thesis. Using the first person in research reports rather than passive voice or impersonal third person has become more widespread, but some professors adamantly oppose it. Get the issue resolved before it turns your defense into a battleground.

Notes

_____

_____

_____

_____

Contribution 33

Betty C. Jung
Southern Connecticut State University

1. *Start early to search for a research topic.*
   Do not wait till the thesis seminar class starts. By the start of the seminar, you should have three topics already chosen, with at least one data collection method in mind for each topic. You should already have some idea about how you would use this data collection method, or if you are thinking of modifying it for your particular research topic. If you are planning to modify, have a good reason for doing so, which is grounded in theory and/or practice.

Average one heading or subheading per page.

Find out early whether you are allowed to use the first person when writing.

Have topics and data collection methods in mind before the thesis seminar class starts.

2. *Do not pick a topic of "personal" interest.*
    Personal interest may cause bias in how you would research a topic. The thesis as an academic exercise should be an objective search for truth. If you feel you may be upset by what the literature shows about your area of interest, then that should indicate that it's time to pick another topic to research. You have to be willing to accept whatever your research finally shows, and if you can't present all your findings because they may conflict with how you want your research to come out, then you are not doing research the way it should be done. This will prepare you for the time when you may be asked to research a topic that may not necessarily be of interest to you but has to be done properly.

    > Consider whether you can live with the findings.

3. *Pick a topic of national relevance in your field.*
    In the field of public health, this is somewhat easy because federal public health agencies have set research agendas, goals, and objectives for the field. For other fields, look to government and professional agencies for areas that can use a graduate student's enthusiasm to look at all sides and then ground results on theoretical models.

    > Consider agencies' research agendas when selecting a topic.

4. *Do not pick a topic of "political" interest.*
    Students need to remember that a "hot" political issue can be forgotten with the next election. If you are going to research an area under hot political debate, think of what your research will say 10 years from now. If it does not have any relevance to the broader area of knowledge you are trying to contribute to, then you have limited yourself to a "white paper" mentality. As an academic exercise, your thesis should add something to the broad body of academic literature, rather than have it used to justify some political stance. If it helps to clarify the issues for debate, that's fine, but the research should not be driven by whether or not the results will be useful for any particular group. If your research can be "used" by "all sides" in the debate, then you are probably doing good research.

    > A "hot" topic today can be a "cold" one later on.

    > Can your research be used by all sides in a debate?

Notes

_____

_____

Contribution 34

David Walker
Iowa State University

Doing a review of the literature can be a time-consuming activity. Usually, students undertake the arduous task of reviewing a source or two at a time through the use of scholarly journals, books, quarterly and annual reviews, or selected abstracts. However, other resources found at many institutions of higher education, the *Dissertation Abstracts International* CD-ROM and the *Comprehensive Dissertation Index* CD-ROM, provide researchers with access to potentially hundreds of dissertation and thesis subjects. In addition, the Internet has a resource called WorldCat, which provides researchers with a means to search libraries throughout the world for a source. Finally, a student's major professor or committee member may mention, on more than one occasion, an obscure source that should be incorporated in the literature review. Often, the professor cannot remember where he or she found out about or received a copy of this magnum opus. Chances are the major professor or committee member had contact with the source at a conference that was supported by a professional organization. Thus, to find a very obscure source, students may want to consult with professional higher education organizations that publish specialized handbooks and monographs.

> Consult the *Dissertation Abstracts International* CD-ROM.

Another frustrating part of the thesis/dissertation process is locating that ever-allusive research instrument that you read about in a journal article but could never locate. A student who would like to reproduce research, but cannot find the original instrument or a modification of the instrument, should consult theses and dissertations. Most of these sources are required to contain either the entire research instrument or a letter to the author of the instrument asking for permission to use it. Either way, the student will find the research instrument or have an address and name for further inquiry.

> Consult theses and dissertations to locate hard-to-find instruments.

Notes

_____

_____

_____

_____

Contribution 35
Surendar Yadava
University of Northern Iowa

There are numerous simple "tricks" a graduate student can take advantage of. Choose a research problem that is quite simple—for example, requiring mainly a descriptive statistical analysis rather than complex statistical analyses such as log linear, factor analysis, and LISREL. For one thing, it is harder for the struggling student to entertain and clarify questions based on complex analyses. Second, a faculty member or a member of a dissertation committee may misunderstand, or worse not understand at all, your analysis, thus ask a wrong question and if the student doesn't answer satisfactorily, get discredited or undervalued. Keep in mind a dissertation is primarily a "requirement" one has to fulfill to obtain a degree, master's or doctorate. It is secondary (or treat it that way) to resolve some pending scientific research issue. Trying to tackle a complex (but interesting) problem may prolong or even shatter the dissertation. One does not have to limit post-dissertation publications and research to one's dissertation or thesis topic. Think of an interesting and "simple" research problem, use secondary data, and analyze them using simple tools such as mean, standard deviation, and correlation.

It is also crucial to have and maintain good working relationships with committee members. Going out with one or more of them for coffee and chatting about your progress will help. It is really helpful to "pick" one member of the committee—other than the thesis director—who knows "little" about the research you are undertaking. But then develop a working relationship with that member familiarizing him or her with your work. Pretty soon he/she will take interest in your work,

Look for a research problem that requires mainly descriptive statistics.

Post-dissertation publications can be on other topics.

Get to know other committee members.

and you can spend more time with that member discussing your writing. In fact, you can indicate to the director that you are spending quite a bit of time with such and such member. That will relieve the major advisor; and not only that, at the time of defense, that friend committee member of yours will speak and advocate on your behalf because most other members would not have read your thesis carefully and will rely on and agree with your "pal."

And it doesn't hurt to offer rides to the committee member once in a while, washing his or her car, or calling on particular occasions such as Thanksgiving to express your gratitude and congeniality. A good strategy and organization are as important as the substance of your research.

Notes

_____

_____

_____

_____

Contribution 36
William G. Iacono
University of Minnesota

Because there is no clear set of expectations for doctoral papers and examinations, I am taking this opportunity to write a friendly memo explaining my personal expectations for these examinations. I am listing here what I consider to be *minimum* requirements, requirements that, if satisfied, will greatly increase the likelihood that your work will be warmly received and favorably evaluated. Your comments and feedback on this document would be appreciated because I expect to revise it from time to time.

If you think it will be necessary to deviate from these requirements, please talk with me in advance about why this is so. Otherwise, I'll assume that you feel these guidelines are reasonable and that it is your intention to abide by them.

Make a friend for the defense.

Butter up the committee members! **(Ha!)**

Some minimum requirements that one professor establishes.

A. *Read and Re-Read This Memo*

Don't plan to read this memo just once and then toss it. Read it upon receipt, again before you begin working on a paper or doctoral exam, and once again before you give me a paper to read. Think of these guidelines as a checklist because that's how I'll be using them. In my review of your work, I will be checking to see to what extent you have addressed each of the points I have raised here. Please don't make the mistake of not taking this memo seriously.

Take written directions from professors seriously.

B. *Scheduling Dates and Times*

1) *Two-week advance notice.* I need a minimum of two weeks to review written work. In many cases, *two weeks will be insufficient.* It is simply neither courteous nor fair that you would expect someone to review your work critically in less than two weeks. If I am your advisor, please expect me to read your paper *before* passing it on to other committee members. After you've revised it by responding to my comments, please give it back to me together with a letter explaining how you've responded and indicating what important changes were made on each page. Once I'm comfortable with your paper, then you can pass it on to other committee members.

Allow at least two weeks for a review of written work.

Have your advisor review it *before* giving it to other committee members.

2) *Two-hour oral exam.* A *minimum* of two hours should be scheduled for an oral exam. It now appears to be the student's responsibility to get each committee member to commit at least two hours. For many exams, a half hour of "administrative time" is usually needed along with 1-1/2 hours for questions. Please get your committee members to agree to both a starting and ending time for your exam.

C. *Written Work*

These guidelines refer to all written work that you might ask me to review, not just writing for doctoral papers.

1) *General Requirements*

Writing well is one of the most difficult tasks we face. There are very few psychologists for whom good scientific writing comes easily. An acceptable draft (i.e., the draft you present to your advisor for the first time) of a paper will usually require at least one day of writing and rewriting per page of double-spaced, typed text. If you are spending less time than this, you are either very good or producing a poor product (in

Typically, expect to spend at least one day of writing for each double-spaced page.

my experience, the latter is more common).

A common writing problem is that of not making the meaning clear. The following suggestions are offered to assist you with clear writing.

a) The most typical problem I encounter with student papers is being unable to understand the rationale or justification for the work. This problem can be very general in the sense that it may not be clear what your goals or objectives were in writing a particular paper. This is often due to starting the writing process without a thoughtfully constructed outline. It may also be very specific in that there is no justification for sample sizes, the inclusion of certain control groups, the choice of special statistical procedures, etc. In general, the first paragraph of a paper should set out your objectives and explain why the work is important. Then, throughout the remainder of the text, use summarizing sentences and connecting narrative to explain why your approach was *A* rather than *B* or why one step was taken rather than another. The step may involve the use of one experimental method rather than another, or, for specials papers, it may concern *exactly* why a particular area of literature is considered relevant to the general topic under discussion, etc.

Provide a rationale for the work.

b) As a rule, tell the reader what you are going to say, say it, then tell the reader what you've said.

c) Don't discount the importance of the title and the abstract or paper summary. Too often I am given papers to read that have no abstracts or summary and sometimes have no title. Please do not give me such papers. Reading the title and abstract provides immediate clues as to how well written the paper is. A title shouldn't be longer than about 15 words and the more information it conveys, the better. It should be a concise statement of the main topic and identify the variables or theoretical issues under investigation. The content of the abstract at the beginning of the paper (or the summary at the end) are even more important, *probably the most important single paragraph in your paper*. This paragraph tests your power of apprehension and sense of proportion. Here you show me you have decided what's important, how important it is, and what can be left out. Your major hypothesis should be stated and the results of its evaluation presented. If your paper is a literature review, explain your objectives, how you've evaluated the literature, and what your conclusions are. If you have not done a good job with your title and abstract, chances are good that

Titles and abstracts are important.

your paper will be unclear.

d) Try to write to the broadest possible audience. Don't write a paper that only your advisor can really be expected to understand.

e) Define abstract terms. It's very distressing to read a long paper on some topic like stress, arousal, biological markers, illness, outcome, etc. without knowing what the author means when using such terms.

Define important terms.

f) Be brief and to the point. All journal articles and grant applications have length restrictions, so this is a good practice. Good writing is shorter than bad writing. The more you can say with the fewest words, the greater your impact will be. In general, 25–40 pages for a specials paper and 85 pages for the body of a dissertation should be ample.

Good writing is shorter than bad writing.

g) Be thoughtful about how you write the introduction to an empirical paper or the entire paper if it is a review article. Your introduction/literature review should not be a comprehensive review of all the relevant literature. Your review should be thoughtfully selective. It should also not read like an annotated bibliography. Keep in mind what point you are trying to make. It should be clear to the reader why you have covered certain studies or areas of the literature and not others and how each study adds to the conclusion you are leading the reader to. Review the literature in a fair manner to show whether or not your point is supported. Make certain your arguments are clear to the reader. Consider the literature review to be like the summation argument that a lawyer gives to a jury in a trial. Use the literature to establish facts and set the context. The jury (your readers) should be sufficiently persuaded by your evidence and argument to feel comfortable with your conclusions. If you are writing an empirical paper, the rationale for conducting your study should be crystal clear by the end of your Introduction.

A literature review should be thoughtfully selective.

Consider a legal analogy.

h) Never write a Results section of a research report or dissertation that is simply an endless presentation of statistical analyses, tables and figures. Include frequent summaries and transition narrative to provide rationales for the steps taken. Explain complex or unusual statistics so that the uninitiated can understand them. Use words to describe the nature of significant effects. For example, if a two-way interaction is significant, use words (and ideally a figure) to describe it.

The Results section needs summaries and narratives.

i) The Results section of a dissertation should include more information than is typically seen in a journal article. Present means and standard deviations for your variables and thoroughly present the results of statistical analyses. If a complete presentation of this type of information causes the Results section to bog down, move less important results or details of results to tables and/or the Appendix. It is important for you to provide this extra information because it's my job to evaluate how well you've handled the data. I can't do that if I don't know what the data and statistical analyses look like.

Consider moving less important results to tables or an appendix.

j) Use headings and subheadings. As a rule of thumb, passages of text should not exceed 500 words without being set off using headings/subheadings. If the paper is long (more than 30 pages), consider supplying a Table of Contents. This step is mandatory for a dissertation. It will help the reader (and you) understand the organization and flow of your paper.

Supply headings and subheadings at intervals of about every 500 words.

k) If you use more than a few common acronyms, provide an acronym glossary spelling out the abbreviations.

l) Use a consistent style (preferably following APA conventions) throughout your paper.

2) *Prospectus*

Many students seem to have particular difficulty writing a prospectus, probably in part because models of what this document should look like are hard to find. One way to think of a prospectus is that it amounts to a contract between you and your committee. Think of it as a paper written through the method section, but in the form of a proposal, so more rationale and justification must be provided. If you get your committee to approve your prospectus and you do the work as outlined, then the committee is, in my view, obligated to give you your degree (provided you can defend the work). The committee will not write you a blank check. If your plan is vague but nevertheless approved, you run the risk that the committee may decide that what you did was not what they agreed to. For example, they might decide that the design was flawed after the work was done and you may have to take remedial steps, including collecting more data, running more groups, etc. You can help avoid this unfortunate possibility by:

Think of a prospectus as a contract.

A vague prospectus can cause problems.

a) Clearly articulating:

51

i) your rationale. Why does this research desperately need to be done? Why is it crucial?

ii) your research aims and objectives. Make your hypotheses clear. What do you want to learn?

iii) your plan for achieving your aims. Explain *exactly* why it makes sense to do the research as you've indicated. How will your method allow you to answer the questions you've posed? It's easy to pick a method that can provide data consistent with your hypothesis. Your challenge is to come up with methods that stand a good chance of refuting your hypothesis (if it should happen to be false). What does your theory forbid the data to look like?

b) Be specific. Justify your sample sizes (e.g., with power analyses) and the types of groups you plan to include/exclude.

c) Don't waste much space reviewing the literature. Summarize the literature *selectively* and *succinctly* in a few paragraphs. The objective of your literature review should be to support your rationale and perhaps some specialized aspects of your method. Don't make the mistake of investing time and effort writing a comprehensive, detailed literature review for a prospectus.

> Consider using a highly selective literature review for a prospectus.

d) Be brief. There's no reason for any prospectus to be more than 20 pages long (double-spaced). Few should be longer than 10 pages.

e) Don't make the mistake of not writing a title and abstract for your prospectus.

D. *Oral Examinations*

> Oral examinations.

1) *Preliminary oral.* Usually, your preliminary oral is focused on your specials paper and/or your prospectus. However, the official purpose of the exam is to determine whether you are qualified to proceed with your Ph.D. work. Hence, you should expect questions related to your written work. You should have an in-depth understanding of the material covered by your specials paper and prospectus. You should also have mastered the core curriculum in clinical psychology and the area covered by your supporting program. You should be prepared to answer questions appropriate for professionals with general mastery in these areas.

If you have presented your preliminary oral committee with a prospectus, whether or not your prospectus is approved by the committee will have little bearing on whether or not you pass your oral. In particular, it will be possible to pass the exam without the prospectus being approved. This outcome is possible because the "official purpose" of the exam is not to evaluate a prospectus.

2) *Final oral.* By this point, you should quite literally be one of the world's experts in the area represented by your dissertation. This expertise should be evident during your oral defense.

3) *General requirement for orals.* Don't plan to give more than a ten minute overview of your work at the beginning of your oral. Practice your synopsis to keep it under ten minutes.

E. *How This Document Applies to You*

This memo outlines the approach I will take to evaluate doctoral papers and examinations. It does not necessarily represent university, department, or clinical program standards. If you are unhappy with my approach, please understand that I will not be offended if I am ultimately not invited to be on your committee. On the other hand, if I am on your committee, I assume that you agree that it is reasonable for me to hold you to the standards I've outlined above.

Notes

_____

_____

_____

_____

Contribution 37
Anonymous
Tempe, Arizona

Choose a very narrowly defined population, and a very narrow

> You should be one of the world's experts on your dissertation topic during orals and the defense.

issue. Focus on this issue to the exclusion of other issues. Don't wander! Choose a dissertation topic where there is plenty of available information.

Choose your dissertation committee carefully and don't be afraid to change members if the committee or project is not working well.

Choose dissertation members who like you and agree with you philosophically, and who have time for you!

Notes

_____

_____

_____

_____

Contribution 38

Bill B. Peters
Tarleton State University

Purchase a computer-based bibliography program (I have used EndNote Plus®) at the very beginning of your graduate career. Beginning with any of the papers you prepare for your classes, put *every single reference* on it, and use it religiously.

The program should have some customizable fields. Make use of these to support your research. For example, I entered library call numbers, interlibrary loan info, what I need to find, what I had on hand, the general topic area, etc. Then, when I needed to go to the library, I would sort everything I needed by call number, print a list, and then just walk down the library shelves pulling off what I needed.

For interlibrary loan, rather than filling out 120 interlibrary loan requests, I produced a printout with all the data they needed and in the order they needed it.

When writing the final document, the program works with your word processor to insert and format your references, citations, and bibliography according to whatever style you use. And, every citation automatically ends up in your bibliography. No more cross-checking

Use a computer-based bibliography program.

between text and bibliography.

The program is well worth the money and the time spent entering the data.

Notes

_____

_____

_____

_____

Contribution 39
Malina Monaco
Georgia State University

1. Set aside one hour (or more) per day to work on thesis/dissertation. That means no phone, spouse, job, kids, etc.
2. Have a set place where you work so everything you need is right there.
3. Write something every day! Even if it is just a paragraph. Some days you will write much more, and some days a paragraph will be a struggle.
4. If you have a particularly difficult task—outline first then slowly fill in outline of what you want to say. Don't worry about sentences. You can always go back and complete your thoughts.
5. Always write as much as possible on a topic. It is much easier to delete things than to add stuff later.

Notes

_____

_____

_____

_____

Suggestions for writing.

Contribution 40

Margot Holaday
Hattiesburg, Mississippi

My dissertation chair informed me that the possibility of anyone EVER reading my dissertation in its entirety was nil. She said that dissertation committees were like people sitting around a table and eating an elephant: Each person was only interested in his or her own piece. So if I thought that my dissertation had to be a wonderful scientific contribution that would change the way people viewed the world, I needed to adjust my expectations, relax, and JUST DO IT.

Dissertation committees eat elephants! (Ha!)

Notes

_____

_____

_____

_____

Contribution 41

Mary Beth Rauktis
University of Pittsburgh

Time Management

I was working about 20 hours a week at a "paying" job while I wrote my dissertation. I decided that even though I would not get paid for the time I put into my dissertation, I was still going to treat it like a "real" job. I decided that a minimum 20 hours a week would be a reasonable amount of time for me to spend on it, and that I could work the 20 hours any way that I liked—two ten-hour days or five four-hour days, etc. I kept a calendar/log where I marked down the amount of time that I spent, and I totaled it each week to make sure that I met my minimum time. I didn't need to write during that 20 hours: The time was legitimate as long as it related to the dissertation, such as reading, making telephone calls, committee meetings, etc. I found this to be helpful because first, it showed the progress that I made. Even if I

Treat your dissertation work like a "real" job.

didn't get much written, I could look at the log and see the time that I spent. It was also helpful because I have a tendency to overwork. If I wanted to do something nondissertation related, I could do it without guilt because I had put in my minimum time. If I wanted to work more than 20 hours, fine, but I had at least put in my minimum time.

I like to write in long stretches of time, and working at my "paying" position sometimes made it hard to write in the evening. I arranged my work schedule so that I could work at my "paid" position Tuesday, Wednesday, and Thursday and then work on my "dissertation job" Friday through Monday. However, I know of many part-timers who got up early in the morning and wrote every day before work, so I guess it is an individual thing. You need to assess how you like to write and try to work a schedule around that preference.

The Politics of a Dissertation

A dissertation is as much a political process as it is an academic exercise. It is worth the time to carefully select your committee. Ask around—are these individuals known to spend time with students, how have they worked with other students? Do any members dislike each other? Do they hold opposing views?

In retrospect, I would have spent more time working with my committee, particularly the individual who was not from my department. I would have kept all of the members better informed of my progress, circulated drafts more frequently, and basically hung around the department more. There is a tendency to "dig in" and write in isolation, but that is not a politically astute thing to do.

Notes

_____

_____

_____

_____

Do other things without guilt—if you've put in the time.

Ask around when selecting committee members.

Working in isolation is not politically astute.

Contribution 42

Paul D. Starr
Auburn University

All writers encounter "writing blocks," particularly those writing a thesis or dissertation. One way to overcome the problem is to break the work into small sections, such as chapters and, in turn, into sections of chapters. If a section is difficult to write, the student may find another topic to treat that feels easier to address. Another tip is to start writing as if one were explaining one's work to a well-educated friend in a letter. The image of a familiar and sympathetic reader often facilitates the task.

Use the image of a familiar and sympathetic reader.

Notes

Contribution 43

Jill Franke
Iowa State University

One of the best suggestions that I received had to do with organization. Someone told me that when I photocopied articles early on and throughout the graduate school process, I should attach a sheet of paper to each article and make notes as to the general content of the article, the theoretical viewpoint, the findings, and any instruments used. Those cover sheets saved me skimming through mountains of articles or retracing my steps to find "the name of that one instrument that I remember reading about two years ago that would be perfect if only I could remember the title!"

Attach a sheet of paper with notes to photocopied articles.

The other tip that I have is to spend some time getting to know your word processing software. Many of the programs have amazing features that will save hours of tedious work trying to format the text to meet university manuscript requirements. Many of the requirements

Get to know your word processing software.

fall outside of the usual range of word processing skills and will give you fits if your current expertise is limited to cutting, pasting, and spacing using the tab key.

Notes

_____

_____

_____

_____

Contribution 44
Thomas A. DeVaney
Southeastern Louisiana University

Start early. Find out about the dissertation/thesis process. Talk to your major professor/advisor about timelines, departmental policies, formats, and anything else you can possibly think of. If your major professor does not want to talk about it, then find another professor who will. This may also be an indication that you do not want this person to serve as the director of your dissertation/thesis since you will be meeting with him or her a lot.

Find out if your program committee will also serve as your dissertation/thesis committee. If so, it is especially important that you select faculty members who get along with each other. It will not help if you get to the proposal or defense stage and members of your committee are arguing because they don't like each other or have completely different views. If you are not familiar with the faculty, question students about who does and does not get along. Or, you could ask your major professor/advisor to prepare a committee and let you approve it. Hopefully, they won't include faculty with whom they do not get along. Furthermore, they will probably select faculty that they have served with before so they may be able to provide some insights about the expectations of the other committee members (which may save a revision or two).

As soon as the committee is selected, begin searching for a topic.

Ask your major professor to recommend committee members.

You might even ask members of your committee. Sometimes they will suggest a topic, which will save a lot of extra legwork.

Start working on a mini-proposal or an outline of your study so that you can start getting feedback. This way it won't be as much of a surprise when they make so many suggestions in your proposal meeting.

When you are preparing for your proposal meeting or defense, talk to your dissertation/thesis director to find out the format of the meeting, how long your presentation should be, whether or not you should have visuals, if you should dress casually or "coat-and-tie," whether to provide refreshments, etc.

Whether it is at the master's or doctoral level, in order to get an early start on the dissertation/thesis, you must have some knowledge concerning the research process. This means you should take the required research courses early in the program. This will not only allow you to decide which type of research you are interested in (e.g., qualitative or quantitative, survey, experimental, etc.) but will also provide the basic knowledge necessary for understanding research articles for the review of literature. Additionally, it will offer you the opportunity to write a proposal. If you get started early, you may even be able to use the topic and proposal from the research class as the basis for your dissertation/thesis.

In the end, there are two main suggestions: a) start early and b) be prepared and know what to expect at every stage in the process.

> Ask committee members to suggest a topic.
>
> Start with a mini-proposal.
>
> Find out what is expected at the proposal meeting or defense.
>
> Take the required research courses early in your program.

Notes

_____

_____

_____

_____

Contribution 45

Johanna F. La Feandra
Dawling College

Plan a time each day for working on the dissertation. Plan something enjoyable right afterwards. Do not excuse yourself easily from the task.

Do not allow yourself to miss important family and social events because you need to work. The work then becomes a torture.

Keep a calendar and mark off each day that you have worked. Seeing the progress graphically helps keep you going.

Don't let it become torture.

Mark off days on a calendar.

Notes

Contribution 46

Charles L. Mitchell
Grambling State University

Dissertation writing requires a complete commitment to rewriting the project. There is no problem that cannot be resolved by a willingness to cheerfully rewrite. Reproduction of a fresh copy of the dissertation reassures all that the project is on target and that there is scholarly ferment in the graduate student's activities.

Cheerfully rewrite!

Notes

Contribution 47

D. Peck
William Paterson University

My dissertation became much more manageable when I realized it was the equivalent of writing ten 20-page papers. That, of course, is not the form it took, but I was so comfortable with that form it helped me realize I could complete the writing in a finite period of time.

Think of it as the equivalent of ten 20-page papers.

Notes

_____

_____

_____

_____

Contribution 48

Virginia Thompson
West Virginia University

Some Advice on Selecting Your Research Topic

As you select your topic and focus your research, be sure to maintain a good perspective on your most immediate goal: completing this particular research project to meet degree requirements. Although choosing a topic that would provide you with many more research opportunities and publications throughout your professional career might seem ideal, that particular goal might be a little too large to be realistic, at least in part because it is rather difficult to predict the future, especially in a world that is changing as rapidly as the one in which we are living. For example, in some fields, even the most "cutting-edge" research can quickly and unexpectedly become obsolete with the appearance of someone else's new publication, or, more important, you might later discover a need and desire to redirect your research interests to relate more specifically to your subsequent professional appointments. Remember that in academia you will (and will be expected to!) continue to develop professionally and, although

Considering the future may not be the key to topic selection.

62

you need to be passionate enough about your dissertation topic to enjoy the investment of time and effort that will be required to do it well and get it done, you will have the rest of your professional career to pursue your research passions. Trying to select a topic according to such longer-term criteria could cause you to invest a disproportionate amount of time at that task and get "bogged down" (a common and frustrating research malady best avoided) right at the beginning. Carefully choose and limit your project to something you will complete in a reasonable and fairly predictable amount of time.

"To Thine Own Self Be True"[1]: Advice on Writing Your Dissertation

"Know thyself."[2] Figure out your strengths and weaknesses and know what it will take for you to get your dissertation done. Keep reminding yourself that this research project is not only something that you have to do, but also something that you are choosing to do in order to reach some long-term goals.

Consider your own strengths and weaknesses.

The following paragraphs describe things that worked for me. Maybe some of them will work for you, or will at least inspire you to come up with your own strategies.

Because of other professional obligations, I had only two days a week plus a third day every other week that were scheduled for writing, but they were indeed *reserved* and guarded with great zeal. The rigidity of this scheduling permitted me to properly "psych" for each bout and also alleviated the fairly typical tendency toward obsessive guilt about not writing *all the time*, which is something that most people really can't do anyway. It also gave my research advisor a more regular and predictable schedule for scribbling all over my drafts with his red ink pen.

Put your advisor on a regular schedule. (Ha!)

On writing days, I would get up, put on the coffee, and go to my desk in my bathrobe. I could dive right in because I always left myself very copious notes on where I had left off and exactly what I needed to do next. This was an important strategy for getting me going without wasting time, and often the first task was to proofread the stuff immediately preceding where I was going to start writing again. I always liked to pour out whatever sentence fragments, thoughts, etc. had been floating around in my head all week and, thanks to the modern miracle of word processing, could then organize, develop, or discard them at a more leisurely pace once they had all been captured.

Make notes for your next writing session.

---

[1] Shakespeare, *Hamlet*.
[2] Anonymous. Inscribed on the temple of Apollo at Delphi. (*The Oxford Dictionary of Quotations*.)

The phone never interrupted me because those were the days of connecting to a mainframe by modem. If I'd had to type the darn thing, I don't think it would've gotten done, but I also wonder how many hours I wasted trying to get the program to format correctly according to the requirements of the Graduate College. The only way I could see the actual formatting was to walk or drive across town to the computer center to pick up a printout. By the completion of the project, my stack of drafts on that oversized computer paper was several feet tall, and I had planned to burn it all with great pomp and circumstance in the fireplace. Of course, when I discovered how long that might actually take, my conscience and practicality took over, and I trucked it to the recycling bin.

Anyway, as I worked, I would make lists of research tasks on which to follow up during the week, marking the sections of the draft that initiated the tasks, so that I could find them quickly when I returned to them the next week. Whenever I got stuck or tired, I would chip away at the more clerical or technical aspects of the document, consulting my lists of those tasks to be done. I'm a list-writing person anyway, but this means of maintaining organization was absolutely vital for my pacing, progress, and sanity. The greatest challenge was to write my lists so that I could actually read them.

The writing days' schedules were as open-ended as possible because I don't like to watch the clock when I'm writing, and I would stop when I found a good stopping place somewhere near my limit of bearable fatigue. Of course, this meant that I was sometimes still in my bathrobe at 5:00 P.M., but—hey—I got my paper done. Fetching a printout often brought closure to the writing day (and a reason to finally get dressed), but sometimes that little break gave me a second wind of which I felt compelled to take advantage.

Somehow, at some point, the project reached completion, and I again started doing laundry and dishes before I ran completely out of clean ones. I don't recall that particular period very clearly, perhaps because I was a little numb; and now, however many years later, I suspect that I've "blanked out" my recollections of the most horrifying aspects of the whole experience so that just the fonder memories remain. The point is, though, that there *are* fond memories. Don't forget: We *choose* to write dissertations. If you decide that the dissertation really isn't "worth it," then don't do it; do something else.

While the preceding details of all my strategies may be totally irrelevant to you because what you need to get the job done is very different from what I needed, I believe there are a couple of underlying fundamental concepts that could be helpful. One is to set

Recycle; don't burn! **(Ha!)**

When stuck or tired, work on clerical or technical aspects.

Out of the bathrobe. **(Ha!)**

There will be fond memories.

small and specific enough goals so that you are usually succeeding rather than failing (e.g., working on a regular schedule, so that if you actually *do* some work at that time, you're *succeeding*; or working through very specific lists of small research tasks). Another is to always start with what you *can* do, and work toward what you are attempting to do (e.g., jotting down a sentence fragment rather than waiting until you have formulated the perfect and complete paragraph, or proofreading a section to reactivate your train of thought). Last, "Let not the sun go down upon your wrath."[3] Try not to end any writing session with a sense of failure or frustration. When you are too tired or too stuck to think any more, complete a technical task so that you can end your session with success. After all, the little successes will keep you coming back for more! Happy writing.

Start with what you can do, and work toward what you are attempting to do.

"Let not the sun go down on your wrath."

Notes

_____

_____

_____

_____

Contribution 49

Rich Robbins
Washburn University

First, if you can, always schedule your committee meetings and your meetings with your chair in the late morning—at 10:30 or 11:00. Faculty members are rarely willing to pass up or even be late for lunch, so you are more likely to have short, focused meetings that end by noon!

Second, when sending out work for review, never simply ask committee members to read it and get back to you. They are busy with other things, and although finishing your work is your top priority, it is not likely theirs. Include a note to the effect of "If I do not hear back from you with any suggested changes, ideas, etc., by [give them a

Schedule for a short, focused meeting with your chair.

[3] The Bible: Ephesians 26.

specific date], I will assume that you are fine with my work the way it is and will continue on." Put a deadline on things, otherwise you will be trying to track your committee members down.

Third, put aside 15 minutes every day to work on your thesis or dissertation. The hard part is scheduling the time and actually sitting down and getting started. Once you do, however, those 15 minutes will often turn into longer periods of time, and before you know it, you will have accomplished so much!

One final suggestion is based on a true event that happened to a friend of mine. He had an emeritus faculty member on his committee who went into surgery for a hip replacement but whose heart stopped during surgery. The retired faculty member died, and my friend was left searching for a replacement committee member a year into his dissertation. Fortunately, the deceased professor was not his committee chair, but what if he had been? The moral of the story is that if at all possible, never ask an emeritus faculty to sit on your committee! What if he or she dies in the middle of your project?

An emeritus faculty member may be a mistake.

Notes

_____

_____

_____

_____

Contribution 50
Michael R. Maples
University of Iowa

One of the most time-consuming parts of the dissertation or thesis is data collection. Accessing a sample and collecting data are two things that can prevent a student from graduating in due time.

After you have chosen your topic and narrowed variables of interest, look for preexisting data sets. I suspect that data is all around you and few people realize it. Ask faculty and another staff who may be active researchers. Perhaps you yourself have collected data for another project that could easily be used for your current research.

Look for preexisting data sets.

This is likely to be true if your dissertation is an extension of your master's or master's equivalency project. Look at local, state, and national agencies to see if they have relevant data sets you could use. Local teaching hospitals, state and federal government departments of education, and even counseling centers may have suitable data. National testing and research organizations, such as American College Testing, may be another possibility. Prisons and even mental health institutes are also places you may want to look. I even know of one psychologist in private practice who has a substantial data set perfect for students doing neuropsychological research. Obviously, sites involved in ongoing research and/or clinical assessments are your best bet.

A few words of caution here. First of all, make certain that the existing data is current. Second, be cognizant of the many relevant ethical codes and principles, such as (but not limited to) research, data sharing, confidentiality, informed consent, and assessment. Finally, do not let the existing data set determine your study. No matter how tempting it is. You probably should not do a study on nursing home adjustment just because your advisor has some data sitting around waiting to be delved into. Develop a study that interests you and then find the data. Remember, even if you have data in hand, you must still do literature reviews, statistical analyses, and a discussion section, so pick a topic that you enjoy studying and can hold your interest. Above all, keep in mind that using an existing data source is a tool for completing your project, one that should be of personal interest and meet some need in the field of study.

Notes

_____

_____

_____

_____

Do not let existing data determine your study.

Contribution 51

Robert Claus
University of Northern Iowa

Do not embark on a research problem about which you know more than your dissertation committee. Especially in social sciences, being simplistic can be a very useful attribute. Make your research sound and methodologically solid. During the writing phase, start by doing a 'sloppy' job. That is, make grammatical and nontechnical errors in writing to the degree that your advisor keeps "busy" while reading and correcting those minor errors without thinking you do not know what you are doing. If you do a perfect job in writing and everything is self-explanatory, your advisor may not think "You are OK and ahead"; instead, the committee members, especially the thesis chair, will think of something that may be unnecessary or complicated for you to undertake. Do an elaborate literature review, and make sure you cite the current and past research in your dissertation area often during your meetings with the committee to give the impression you are articulate and thorough in your work—hence, that will cut down the chance of them asking trivial and irrelevant questions of you. It will be very helpful to somehow incorporate or cite the work of one or more of your thesis committee faculty members. Just drop by the office of a faculty member and have an impromptu chat about your research agenda—both current and post graduation. Creating a good impression, playing the role properly, and going by the rules help. Remember, at the time of defense, the members will make use of the impression and information you have provided them during prior months or years.

At the time of defending your thesis, choose a time when most faculty are busy and won't bother to attend your presentation. That is helpful because the more audience you have, the higher the chance of someone asking a question you may not be able to answer or answer wrong and that might give a wrong impression to others. The Dissertation Presentation is not a court hearing in front of a judge or jury. So be articulate and elaborative by taking more time than necessary in answering a question. It is not too difficult to take two or more hours in addressing only a few questions. That will "intimidate" others and keep them from asking you more questions because you are so "thorough" and know what you are talking about. Remember, "What you say is important, but *how* you say it is equally important." Saying too much will usually mean "you are on top of things." And submit your written work to the committee just on time rather than in

---

Some tongue-in-cheek advice!

Keep your advisor busy with grammatical and nontechnical errors. **(Ha!)**

Take two or more hours to answer a few questions during your defense. **(Ha!)**

plenty of time.

Notes

_____

_____

_____

_____

Contribution 52

Marai Yaw
University of Central Florida

Completing a dissertation can be a lonely undertaking. You will need several support systems.

Your support systems should include:

1. An *emotional* support system. Don't wait until things get tough. Recruit your family, if possible. Let them know your special needs and ask for their help. Nourish them in their support efforts when things are going right, and they will be more likely to be there for you when the going gets tough. Actually think about, and plan how to make them active participants in your success. Celebrate the milestones with them and make them feel that they have played an active role at each level.

Not all of you will be lucky enough to have a family who will give you *all* the support you need. Even if your family is supportive, you will need someone outside of your immediate family to help you keep a sense of perspective. Recruit a friend who knows your strengths and weaknesses and who will support you but also help you straighten yourself out when you get off track. Know what kind of support helps you most in other endeavors and plan to have that kind of support for this journey. Take time to appreciate and nurture the giver!

Anticipate people or events that might have a negative effect on your emotional state as you progress through the program. Anticipating the negatives allows you to disarm them in advance. Direct confrontation is usually ineffective or actually

Don't wait until things get tough to establish an emotional support system.

counterproductive. People who are negative about your efforts are usually reflecting their own fears, personal frustrations, or jealousy. Some family members might resent your intense involvement in the dissertation process. They feel a loss. Refuse to see negative attitudes as personal attacks. Fall back on your external emotional support system to help you deal with the negatives in a positive way. Validate hurt feelings but do not accept guilt feelings as a result. Try and reach a compromise that allows everyone to have *some* of their needs met, including you.

Dealing with people who are negative about your efforts.

Be prepared if part of your planned system of support seems to fail now and then. Discouragement at times is part of the process. It can even be a symptom that you have reached the point to *stop* worrying about whether your dissertation is exactly right and get it finished.

Don't hesitate to get help if you *do* get overwhelmed. Sometimes an objective view of the whole picture by a professional can open possibilities you never considered. Most universities have counseling services available to students through health services.

Get professional help if you are overwhelmed.

2.   You will also need an *educational* support system. Perhaps the easiest, ongoing way to develop such a system is through a cohort study group. Make the group as diverse as possible, but try to form or join a group with an overall positive outlook. See yourselves as problem solvers with different strengths who can help each other. The weakest member of the group can turn out to be the most valuable. In helping a weak member succeed, you will gain valuable insight into the processes you need to succeed yourself.

The weakest member of a cohort group can be the most valuable.

Recruit professors to help solve problems or act as mentors for the group. Don't ask too much of them, because time is a precious commodity; however, timely help from a professional can help enormously. If you have made contact with a professor in advance, laying out the goals of the group, you are more likely to get help if you really need it.

Investigate the extra facilities available to students on campus. Many have special services for students. They may or may not have exactly what you need, but they may be able to help you set it up. Frequently, they will team students together so that an experienced student can guide an inexperienced student. A doctoral candidate who has progressed through most of the dissertation process can be a valuable mentor.

A doctoral candidate nearing completion may make a valuable mentor.

Make friends with the research librarian both at the university library and at your local library. Searching the literature effectively has become a huge problem. The availability of on-line searches has brought much more information within reach, but finding just what you need among such a huge volume of both relevant and irrelevant work is a task that requires professional help. Good research librarians have many techniques for narrowing a search. Don't neglect the old paper searches. Some of the most valuable references can be the result of serendipitous finds while looking for something else. This doesn't happen often with an electronic search.

Ask professors to recommend current research papers from previous students. Spend considerable time looking at dissertations filed in the library. Note what you like and what you dislike. Try making a model of your ideal dissertation based on this research, and use that model in planning your own dissertation.

3. A *financial* support system is also a necessity for many of you. Going through the doctoral program can be an expensive undertaking, and it is not always easy to find financial support at this level. Books and services are available to help you find grants at the doctoral level. Searching for financial assistance requires some dedication. Set aside sufficient time and effort to search for aid. Keep hunting and don't give up if you don't succeed at first. The big grants are hard to get, but there are many small grants available that can add up to a substantial sum.

The university may have money available through offices other than financial aid. Most universities have an office concerned with sponsored research. You will need to work closely with a professor, usually your principal advisor, but you might find that you can get the cost of the dissertation underwritten by an outside company.

Think about the possibility of getting specific parts of your work underwritten by your current employer. Many employers who will not pay the entire cost of an employee's education *are* willing to pay the costs of one element, copying for instance. Others might pay for textbooks. Small, specific requests are more likely to be met than big ones, but it is often the small, unanticipated expenses that seem the most onerous. If your employer is playing an active part in your progress, however small, he or she is more likely to support you when you need extra consideration during the degree process.

Set up a "Support System Slush Fund" as soon as you commit to an advanced degree program. Be creative, collect loose change, save the cost of a cup of coffee, have a garage sale, etc. Small amounts add up over time. Use this slush fund to support yourself in small but necessary ways without feeling guilty about taking money from the household budget.

No one can anticipate all the problems that will come along while working towards an advanced degree. By having support systems in place to anticipate the common problems, you *can* avoid being overwhelmed when unexpected difficulties arise. Most students don't quit because of one big problem, but because of the cumulative effect of smaller problems and because of increased isolation as you become engrossed in the process. By nurturing your support teams from the beginning, you will build connections rather than lose them in the intense effort required to succeed at the advanced levels. By including others in your plans, you are more likely to keep on track and finish because you will feel a commitment to those who help you.

Notes

_____

_____

_____

_____

| | Beware of the cumulative effect of small problems. |

Contribution 53
Carolyn M. Byerly
Ithaca College

1. Keep the project and research narrowly focused and manageable. Avoid large-scale projects at all costs! Select an advisor who agrees to such.
2. Also keep the literature related to the research focused.
3. Remember that your dissertation advisor is the administrator of your committee—let this person troubleshoot and coordinate for you. Avoid putting yourself in the position of negotiating with several members of your committee over fine points. Let the advisor be the gatekeeper and hold her/him to this responsibility.
4. Define your own area of research. Avoid doing a project your advisor (or other faculty) thinks should be done.
5. Try to keep balance in your life—sleep regularly, exercise, eat

| | Let your dissertation advisor troubleshoot and coordinate. |

well, see friends, and see a movie sometimes.

Notes

_____

_____

_____

_____

Contribution 54
Donald Lee Stovall
University of Wisconsin, River Falls

The writing process is a basic part of developing a dissertation. For many students, one area where improvement can be gained involves their understanding and use of technology to help them with the writing process. If students can learn to use technology, they will find that they can give more attention to the content of their dissertation, and ultimately make it stronger.

Many students are either intimidated by technology, or fail to use technology to their advantage. In my experience with students, many of them, for example, fail to use the most beneficial aspects of their word processing programs. In their haste to get ideas down on paper or to produce a document for review, many students develop only an elementary understanding of their word processing programs. There are, however, several components found in many of the popular word processing programs that, if properly used or understood, would ultimately streamline the writing process and allow students to focus more on the ideas and issues they wish to communicate to their audience.

Many students will state that they do not have the time to study their word processing manual. Others will state that they cannot spend the time to follow on-line tutorials that come with word processing programs. However, the investment of a few hours reviewing manuals or following tutorials could save many more hours of frustration involved with struggling to edit, recompose, or organize a document.

The importance of thoroughly understanding a word processing program.

A few hours reviewing a manual could save much time later.

There are numerous word processing features available to the author of a dissertation. Some examples include cut and paste, automatic correction of words that are frequently misspelled by the author, thesaurus programs, or programs which assess the grammar and readability of the document. Learning how to use these features, and others, allows the student to develop documents that contain few writing errors (errors associated with interpretation of data is another matter). Other features, such as mail merge, can save time if one is preparing information for a list of recipients.

There is a downside to technology that requires vigilance on the part of the student. I have had frantic students under stress reporting that their disk drives have crashed or that their computer and printer have stopped communicating, so that they are unable to get documents out of their computer. For these times, automatic backup of information on a scheduled basis becomes an important feature. The computer, as a tool, is only useful if one understands how it can be helpful. Understanding features imbedded within one's word processing program is only one aspect of technology. Other aspects include issues such as scanners, word recognition programs, or the Internet. A quality word processing program can become the program that ties together all of these options for the person engaged in research.

Word processing.

Notes

_____

_____

_____

_____

Contribution 55
James J. Green
St. Thomas Aquinas College

Recognize the need for discipline and prioritization as to completing your project. It is an all-encompassing effort and must be approached accordingly. Internal discipline as to effort and time frames is necessary, as is a top-flight priority consciousness which enables one to continually place the endeavor in first place.

Notes

_____

_____

_____

_____

Contribution 56
Anonymous
Blacksburg, Virginia

Perhaps relating an actual experience I had during the dissertation process will help. A friend of mine was doing a dissertation on a famous philosopher. He had gathered as much information as possible on this philosopher. There were articles in numerous foreign languages, articles about the philosopher, critiques of the philosopher, and so forth.

Each time he sat down to write, someone or another would appear at his door and say to him, "Say, have you seen the latest issue of [insert name of the most obscure journal you can find]? There's another article on this philosopher." He would drop everything he was doing, find the article, and have it translated, if necessary. Usually this process would take several months. Then, he would start to write once more. At that point, someone else would appear at the door and the process would begin again. To the best of my knowledge, he had not written a single word in seven years when I left the university to take my first job. I lost track of him at that point.

I always advise graduate students that they must stop their research process at some point and simply begin. If you are constantly stopping the process to find the next new twist on the topic, you will never get started. I believe this is the same advice contained in the phrase, "It's time to either fish or cut bait."

I hope this incident will be of some use. Please don't use my name because someone might figure out who this fellow was. I really

An endless search for information.

Fish or cut bait.

don't want to cause him any embarrassment.

Notes

_____

_____

_____

_____

Contribution 57
Scott A. Myers
Creighton University

Tip #1

While this tip may appear trivial and common sensible, I can honestly say that it helped me complete my dissertation on time. The tip is simple: Schedule blocks of time during which you do nothing but dissertation work. This work can include researching, writing, typing, copyediting, checking references, inputting data, analyzing data, and thinking/reflecting. Because of my busy schedule in graduate school, I allotted three days per week solely for dissertation work. This does not mean that I spent only three days a week on the dissertation—it means that there were three days that could be used for nothing *but* dissertation work. For example, during my last year in graduate school, I segmented my activities into specific days so that I could get the most use out of my time. Tuesdays and Thursdays were spent fulfilling my assistantship duties; Wednesdays were devoted to fulfilling my duties as an officer of the Graduate Student Senate. This left Monday, Friday, and Saturday as my designated "dissertation days." On each of these days, I would spend from 8:00 A.M.–5:00 P.M. working on some aspect of the dissertation. Regardless of the stage of the dissertation at which I was, I would fill this time block by working on something, or anything, related to the dissertation. If I finished my delegated tasks for the day and had time left, I did something else related to the dissertation. For instance, if copyediting one of the chapters took only six hours, then I would spend the rest of the time typing these changes. Rather than putting tasks off, I plunged in

Consider setting aside "dissertation days."

76

immediately. And when the clock read 5 P.M., I stopped my task—regardless of what still needed to be finished. In addition, during these "dissertation days," I did not allow myself to get involved in other tasks. For example, any class prep or grading for the course I taught as a graduate assistant had to be done on either Tuesday, Thursday, or in the evening, but never during the time block designated as a "dissertation day." By sticking to this rigid time schedule, I finished my dissertation on time (actually, I finished ahead of schedule.) I also used this time management schedule for my thesis work and ended up completing my thesis in February—months ahead of my May graduation date.

Tip #2

Along this line, another tip I would suggest is to establish a standing meeting or appointment time with your advisor. The realization of this tip may be contingent upon your advisor's schedule, but a regularly scheduled meeting time can be a lifesaver for multiple reasons. My advisor and I established a standing meeting time of 4:00–5:00 P.M. every Thursday. This predetermined meeting time had several benefits. First, it guaranteed a time period—a valuable commodity in graduate school—where the focus was deliberately centered around the dissertation. Second, it offered a time period where my advisor and I could discuss any other issues unrelated to the dissertation. Third, it provided a time period that enabled me to ask any questions or solicit feedback. Because I had this standing meeting time established, whenever I had a question or concern as I was working on the dissertation, I wrote the question/concern down and addressed it during the meeting, rather than running to the phone every time a question arose or trying to find my advisor whenever I had a concern. The standing meeting allowed both my advisor and me to maximize our time. There were also several weeks when we didn't meet, mainly because I didn't have problems, or when we met for 20 minutes. The bottom line is that the standing meeting time can be helpful in that you know there is always a specific amount of time set aside for you and your dissertation.

> Try to establish a standing meeting time with your advisor.

Notes

_____

_____

_____

_____

Contribution 58

Donna Pawlowski
Creighton University

I think the most important suggestions for students completing graduate work are to have a positive working relationship with your advisor (and committee) and to have a committed timeline. First of all, the relationship with the advisor is vitally important to the success and completion of any thesis or dissertation. My relationship with my advisor was such that she would have materials turned around within three days of receiving them. If you show your advisor that you are serious about completing the dissertation and continue to provide her/him with materials to read, s/he is more likely to respond in fashion. In addition to having a good advisor, you should also rely on the expertise of your committee members. Do not just talk to your committee when you drop off parts of the dissertation, but show them that you are interested in their input about your progress. Seek them out for ideas and resources about your project—show them that you really want them involved, not just to sign off on paperwork, but to help generate ideas for your project. Creating a positive relationship with your advisor and committee is half of your success in completing the dissertation!

> Show your advisor that you are serious.

Second, commit to a realistic timeline. Your time for completing the dissertation must include turnaround time from your advisor and committee. Too many times, people anticipate completing the dissertation within "X" number of months. Estimate that from the time you drop off anything to your committee to the time of defense, 6–8 weeks may pass. Working with everyone's schedules may take longer than anticipated. Regardless of the process, most institutions have a two-step defense process; one for the proposal, which includes the method's chapter, and a final defense for the completed dissertation. Make sure you have accounted for each of these in your timeline. So just be patient, create a visual presence for your committee (to remind them that you are still around and would like to be done!), and be understanding of the process.

> Create a visual presence for your committee.

If you follow these few suggestions, your dissertation life will be made easier. It does get frustrating at times; however, just remember they are your advisor and committee, and you should respect their decisions. You may be assertive in your ideas, but know when to back down from your position and accept theirs. You have the rest of your life for scholarship; however, your present behaviors could determine the rest of your life!!

> Be assertive, but know when to back down.

_____

_____

_____

_____

Contribution 59

Anonymous
Los Angeles, California

Here's a story told to me by someone who was at the University of [bleep] when it happened. A grad student defending a thesis put up an overhead of plotted factor scores which showed the desired pattern, except for one recalcitrant subject up in the right quadrant of the plot. When grilled relentlessly by an unsympathetic committee member about the effects of outliers on such solutions, the student responded with a detailed description of how the case had been carefully examined, and every possible explanation considered, resulting in a decision to leave the subject in, especially since it didn't seem to modify the pattern very much after all. Unfortunately for the graduate student, when he turned off the overhead projector, the fly stayed on the wall.

Notes

_____

_____

_____

_____

During the dissertation defense, watch out for outliers!
(Ha!)

Contribution 60
Brian Berry
Holy Family College

Dissertation Recommendations

Above all, schedule time to dedicate to the necessary steps needed to complete the dissertation. Doctoral students have undoubtedly been trained well and are accomplished at doing the required work of a higher education program. However, the structure provided in a 15-week course with specified assignments differs dramatically from the individually self-directed nature of completing the dissertation or thesis. For this reason, it is essential for the doctoral student to build in time and goals, much like those provided in a typical graduate course, in order to move along.

Qualify and organize activities into categories that will allow for momentum to be maintained. For instance, formatting the document on days when you just can't think is good to do to keep the process going and to keep chipping away toward the final product.

Near the Dissertation Defense Time

Don't be intimidated by your position as student versus faculty's role as "expert." Like anyone, faculty on your committee will have more or less expertise in given areas and will also have more or less motivation to attend to your time and work requirements. Make sure you give faculty assignments and timelines for getting feedback to you and that you follow through. Too often, because of prior teacher/student relationships, the doctoral student will not take the initiative to make sure feedback is provided in a timely fashion.

> Take the initiative in getting feedback.

Farm out activities that can be farmed out. This doesn't mean you should just hire someone to do data analysis, for instance. However, some data entry or coding of data may be an activity someone else can do so you can dedicate time for more critical tasks. Just make sure data coding is done correctly.

> Farm out what you can.

Notes

_____

_____

_____

_____

Contribution 61

Elisabeth H. Sandberg
Suffolk University

Before you ever write the first word of your thesis (especially your dissertation), take a day or two to set up your word processor for the task. By defining styles and section formatting in advance, you can type your titles, headings, text, and footnotes in the correct format from the very beginning. This will save you hours of mind-numbing labor at the end.

Set up your word processor for the task.

The second piece of advice I give to thesis writers is to take a "divide and conquer" approach. Setting subgoals—*manageable* subgoals—during the writing process is essential for one's sanity and progress. I'm sure that everyone is aware that you can't sit down one day and say, okay I'm going to write my thesis now; but I still think most students are guilty of biting off chunks that are too large to chew, much less swallow. Do *not* sit down with a plan to write chapter 4, or to write your entire results section. Instead, set small, attainable goals on a daily (or weekly) basis. "Today I am going to edit the intro to chapter 2, and I am going to write the materials section for chapter 3." You will be proud of yourself when you accomplish your goals, and you will avoid feeling overwhelmed by the magnitude of the project.

Divide and conquer.

Finally, I tell students to set aside a specific, yet limited number of hours at the same time every day for writing. I worked on writing my dissertation from 9:00 A.M. to noon every weekday until it was finished. The interval was short enough to stay focused and to avoid fatigue, but long enough to allow for definite daily progress. The regimentation was reassuring—I knew that someday it would be done.

Set a long enough work interval to make definite daily progress.

Notes

_____

_____

_____

_____

Contribution 62

James J. Monahan
University of New Haven

1. Develop a strong and mutually respectful relationship with your advisor or professor.
2. Encourage the development of "research teams" composed of faculty and students in your department.
3. Expand your reading area beyond your interest. Develop a wide reading base. This will stimulate new ideas.
4. Set a *reasonable* library/study/writing schedule on a daily basis as early in your graduate career as possible. Stick to it. Don't cram!!
5. Help out other grad students with their ideas. You tend to get back what you give.
6. Find a topic that you love, or are somewhat passionate about.
7. After #6, talk about it with your professor, other students, significant other, etc. (Don't treat the idea like a virus.) Nurture it.
8. Work on a *simple design* to measure or study a particular aspect of the problem.
9. Find a reasonable statistics consultant for your committee.
10. Don't expect the study to be perfect!

You tend to get back what you give.

Avoid perfectionism.

Notes

_____

_____

_____

_____

Contribution 63

John G. Mehm
University of Hartford

For many students in clinical or counseling psychology, the dissertation process is interrupted or delayed by the year-long internship taken after three or more years of doctoral study. The majority of students on internship find themselves relocating a great

Working on the dissertation while doing an internship.

distance away from their graduate program (our record at the University of Hartford is a student who did an internship in Honolulu). This process is further complicated by the amount of time to move and settle in a new location, adjust to the demands of the internship, enjoy any holidays, look for a post-internship job, repack boxes, and relocate once again.

One of the biggest problems while on internship is keeping in touch with your dissertation advisor on a regular basis. E-mail becomes a useful and inexpensive way to exchange information with an advisor long distance. This is much cheaper for a student than sending the copy by overnight or express mail, which may seem like a good idea for a single use. However, when you consider how many revisions may be required, express mail becomes an expensive proposition. I have supervised several dissertations long-distance, in which the student sends a section of the dissertation by e-mail, and we discuss it by phone a few days later. This method helps the student maintain momentum and make steady progress.

A few tips (which I have learned the hard way) make this process much more workable than it may seem at first. First, instead of sending a section of your dissertation as the e-mail message itself, send it as an attachment to your e-mail cover memo. This will allow you and your advisor to read not only the same text, but the same format and pagination as well. Second, use your page setup functions to number the lines on each page when you send your advisor a draft. Page and line numbers (as I've done here) make it so much easier for both parties to locate a particular passage, which is a major challenge when you're talking by phone. Third, as with any method of advisement, do not conclude a dissertation meeting on the phone without setting up the next meeting and a target for what should be accomplished by then. Without your physical presence on campus, it is just too easy for your project to take a lower priority and allow a large amount of time to pass without any progress.

Working on a dissertation at long-distance.

Advantage of sending text as an attachment via e-mail.

Page and *line numbers* make it easy to communicate, especially on the phone.

Notes

_____

_____

_____

_____

Contribution 64

Daniel J. Mueller
Indiana University

1. Write it down! Rather than meeting with a professor to discuss *orally* some vague idea, *write one or two paragraphs* about the idea. This will help *both the student and the professor* understand the essence of the idea. If it can't be written down in a succinct manner, it's not worth talking about.

2. Often two, three, or four related ideas emerge. Thus two, three, or four separate "prospectuses" should be written. Then, it is often easy, even for the writer, to identify the one or two with best potential.

3. Make appointments (commitments for products). Procrastination is automatic. Progress must be scheduled.

There are several misconceptions and pitfalls that I often see interfering with developing good research questions:

1. Thinking that developing a good research question is primarily a matter of finding the right wording for the question—that there's some "formula" that a question needs to conform to—rather than a primarily substantive matter of what you want to understand. This goes along with the idea that writing a good research question is a matter of methodological expertise rather than specific knowledge of the field and phenomena you want to study.

2. Seeing research questions as the starting point for an investigation and the determinant of all future steps in the investigation, rather than as the result of an iterative process of considering the literature, your own experience with the phenomena you want to understand, your purposes in doing the study, the kinds of data you could feasibly collect to answer your questions, and the potential validity threats to your potential conclusions. See my book[4] for a detailed discussion of this.

3. Confusing research questions with interview or survey questions.

4. Thinking that developing research questions should be a simple, one-pass process, rather than something that requires sustained thinking, repeated revisions, and critical feedback from others.

5. Assuming that research questions should invariably be framed in general terms, rather than being specific to the particular program, setting, or individuals that you plan to study.

Write your ideas down before meeting with a professor.

Consider writing two to four "prospectuses" from which to select.

Misconceptions and pitfalls that interfere with developing good research questions.

---

[4] *Qualitative Research Designs: An Interactive Approach*

84

6. Assuming that research questions should be stated in terms of observable data, rather than referring explicitly to theoretical constructs (i.e., taking a positivist or instrumentalist rather than realist approach).

Notes

Contribution 65
Angeline Lillaro
University of Virginia

Do something every day—even if it's just typing in references.

Notes

Contribution 66
Ryda D. Rose
University of Pennsylvania

For some 31 years now, I have been privileged to work with literally scores of graduate students who are in the process of preparing their dissertations or theses. For some, I have been the Chair

Advice you've seen throughout this book. Consider posting it where you will see it every day.

of the committee; for others, I sat as a member of the graduate group or as a personal advisor. In this, my sabbatical year, there is still a group of 15 students to whom I am committed to advise, to help revise, to see them through to the final defense.

Of course, each student is a unique individual with his/her own capabilities and idiosyncrasies. Some write extremely well and are capable of putting thoughts into appropriate scholarly arguments on the written page. Others, at this level, have the critical thinking skills; but the transferal to the written, clear expression lacks coherence and competency. This second group needs more help than the first group, who, when given some literary devices, can take off and do the job, very much under their own motivations.

Both sets of students need the basic structure to get started with the process. Unless they are working with a professor who has his/her own research program with its own method, they are lost as to where to begin. The research design courses, as good as they are, do not come into a focus that helps a new scholar seek and find his/her own niche.

We begin with the structure. Very often it is merely a command to send the student to the library to do the literature search; to come up with at least three (3) good arguments as to why what s/he wants to study is important for the intellectual and social growth of the research community or humankind, in general. What are its substrates? Who did what, when, how? What gap has to be filled? What implications from a very recent study emerge that point to a rationale for the present undertaking? Why is it important that it be done, now, by you? What contributions will it make to the field, to the existing literature? Where might it lead? Will it be feasible? Can it be done with your existing resources? Whom might you call upon to make sure that it happens?

We plot a Venn-Diagram with at least three (3) circles that intersect. Each of the circles of intellectual study is a recognized area of importance contingent to the projected study. If an argument from each body of literature emerges from each of the three areas, then the intersect is certainly the intended study with strong rationales for its undertaking! When students start this search, using all the electronic search engines now in use, there may be other areas of scholarly concern that come into view. This is the hope. This phenomenon will assure that the foundations for the study are exhaustive and cogent. This is the basis of true scholarship.

Next, and most important—we give a timeline. Students are used to timelines. They have been required all their school lives to "turn a

Two types of students.

Students need structure.

Consider using a Venn-Diagram.

paper in" on a certain date. The doctoral process has no such structure. Very often the professor says, "When you have something, let me see it." That "something," very often, takes a year or two to make its appearance, if it ever does! I give students a time and a date when I would like to see their work. I tell them that I will set that weekend aside to look at their work! This tactic engenders a sense of responsibility and even some "guilt" for them. They know that someone else may have had to wait because they did not show up! A weekend lost, in a sense! For mature graduate students, this ploy works. They often put things "not due" aside while taking care of family and other work responsibilities.

I generally try to convene a cohort of students at the same stage. They take consolation and hope and advice from each other. In former years, I set up a 900-level course, where there was a writing assignment relating to the Problem, the Purpose, the Questions, the Methods—each week. Then each student would present his/her thoughts and get group feedback, not only from me, but from peers. This format is ideal for encouraging attention and constant on-task behaviors.

With the library search completed, the writing begins. In a traditional form of research, this often takes the form of a chapter two. When I receive writing on a Friday, the student can expect a return— the *following week*. This fact is, perhaps, the most salient in ensuring the student's continuing to be on task. Professors who wait months and years to return copy abound. With the moderate load in teaching on most staffs, this is unconscionable behavior. In my mode of action, I have to practice what I preach. If I want a student to get ahead with the project, s/he must have ongoing, timely feedback. As the structure and arguments emerge, I advise the students to meet with other committee/expert members to see whether we are going in the right direction. Is there anything we have missed? Do our arguments make sense?

Then we move on to other aspects of the proposal. I like to have components of every aspect of a study in the proposal. In essence, this looks very much like chapters one (all components, eclipsed); two (literature search and arguments); and, three (the method) in traditional terms. Students who have not reviewed substrates of their projects before the fact are loathe to return to such after the study is done. This modus operandi does not preclude bringing other literature arguments to bear in the final moments. If the results demand new lenses and meanings, of course, we return to the current literature for them and use them in our chapters four's and five's Results, Analyses,

Hope your professor makes you feel guilty!

Put all components into the proposal.

Discussion, Limitations, Conclusions and Implications sections. The method chapter sometimes also is modified as it begins to function in real time and the real world.

There is one big caveat limitation to my above description of how I manage a traditional dissertation advising situation. In some cases there is a crossover to the new naturalistic, qualitative, interpretive modes in contemporary method. Some scholars, however, hesitate to have their students become immersed in the literature of what was, what is. They feel that a bias may be introduced, which could influence perceptions and ensuing interpretations. They would rather have their students just start with nothing, very little background. Fine, for a while, but if there are no substrates on which to rest new observations, how can our new researchers even know that they have something at which to look? Which to analyze? Something that says something? I am amenable to the concept of "bracketing" biases in the beginning of a study. Very few works in the human condition are free of all bias. I would compromise on the extent of the literature search if a committee member were uncomfortable. I would not eliminate it entirely.

Controversy about the literature search.

How I get the students to explore method is also interesting. I have them put their intended study into all current methodological formats. Then as they look at the Purpose and Problem Statements of their work, they must create an argument for or against those methods that will be valid or nonfunctional for their ultimate goals. This exercise is very fruitful not only for tunneling in on their own project, but also gives them ammunition for the oral defense when they are required to support their decision-making outcomes.

Consider your study in all methodological formats.

Thanks for the opportunity to review some of the successful moments of a very fulfilling academic career. Good luck in your publication's efforts in this direction.

Notes

_____

_____

_____

_____

Contribution 67
Gary Taylor
University of Arkansas

Suggestion #1

One of the most difficult distillation processes that students have to go through in dissertation writing is to isolate exactly what their specific statement of the problem is to be. To help solve this difficulty, I have students meet together in small groups (4 to 6 students) where I guide them in a seminar type class. The objective of the class is to have each student present his/her statement of the problem and give a short itinerary as to how they are going to progress through their study based upon the statement of the problem that they currently have.

The other students then ask questions about any difficulties they would have in explaining this study to a third party (me). After the presentation and question-answer period, I will ask one of the second parties to explain somebody else's study and defend it. Questions such as variables, population, time, place, setting, data gathering procedures, even expected results are common types of questions.

The greatest value has always been when the presenter finds that his/her peers have trouble understanding what the study is all about. This becomes a great motivation for causing the student-researcher to give more consideration to the potential reader.

Suggestion #2

I have students fill out what might be called an information graph on their potential study. An information graph is simply a way to organize information into categories. The graph which I have found most useful for thesis and dissertation students is one formed around the types of questions which are generally asked about any body of knowledge:

The "wh" questions"

What is your study about?
Where does it take place?
When does it take place?
Who is involved?

Then:
Why is such a study of value to the body of knowledge?
How are you going to do it?

Students will answer each of these questions about their study at

> A seminar on the process may help.

> Answering the *"wh"* questions when planning.

the proposal stage. Later, I will have them present their proposed study to other peer students and these peer students will answer these same questions after listening to the presentation.

Finally, just before the candidates are ready to prepare for the final defense of their study, I will have them answer these same types of questions, which helps them to see what they have learned from the process of the study itself. The information graph itself builds great confidence in the students that they have done a good study, and it helps me to have a kind of quick summary of what the students are doing in their study.

Suggestion #3

As candidates prepare for both their defense and their final copy of their study, I will have them go to a very large private room or hallway and lay all the pages of their manuscript out in sequence on either the floor or on tables. They then check to see: (1) Does the table of contents agree with the manuscript sequence, wording for titles, tables, page numbers, major sections, and illustrations? Is it all there as advertised in the table of contents? (2) Are all the appropriate parts together at their "designated meeting places?" (3) For every question, hypothesis, or stated purpose listed in chapter one is there a place where data gathering has been identified, analyzed, summarized, and conclusions made at the end of the study?

I remind my students that their professors dedicated half their lives to getting their doctoral degrees, and that they have dedicated the other half of their lives to making sure that no one else gets one.

Notes

_____

_____

_____

_____

Lay it all out for a final check.

Dedicated to making sure you never get one.
(Ha!)

90

Contribution 68

Marios S. Pattichis
Washington State University

Marios' Tips on Finishing the Dissertation

1. If you take your work too seriously, you may not be as productive as you want to be. After spending hours trying to start the dissertation slides in a file called phd_defense.tex, I typed and finished my defense slides in a file called play.tex, which was thought to be a scratch file for writing down basic ideas.

2. It pays to be your own worst critic, instead of having your committee members "fish" for the problems with your dissertation.

3. "Leave the Nobel Prize-winning work for later. Do not try to do that in your dissertation." I take to heart this advice given to me by Professor Athanasios Papoulis: Avoid taking your dissertation too seriously—that it will change the world, etc.

4. Avoid being very creative when you write the results. Instead, recognize that certain things need to be said even though they may not sound very original.

5. Keep a fixed schedule so that you work consistently on the dissertation.

6. If you are concerned about numerous corrections to your dissertation, simply minimize your responses to each committee member.

Don't take yourself too seriously.

Leave the Nobel Prize for later.

Avoid being overly creative when writing the results.

Notes

_____

_____

_____

_____

Contribution 69

Sylvia Celedón-Pattichis
Washington State University

Sylvia's Tips for Finishing the Dissertation

If you are like me, you are probably planning a wedding, hoping to defend the dissertation, and planning a move immediately after you have completed all requirements for the degree to begin a new job as assistant professor. As you well know, all of these events are rated as high levels of stress in life. I hope the advice below helps alleviate some of that stress.

My suggestions for students working on theses or dissertations are:

1. Think of a possible dissertation topic as soon as you begin your program, and develop your dissertation from papers submitted for coursework, especially the review of the literature.

2. If necessary, complete the forms for the human subjects committee (e.g., consent forms, etc.). Pilot your study as soon as possible so that you know which areas of the study need improvement. If the dissertation turns out to be of the same nature as your pilot study, you may not have to resubmit the paperwork to the human subjects committee. Simply give them an update of your study. Ask for this option at your institution. If you are working in school settings, submit paperwork to obtain permission from them as early as possible. Any delay in this process may also delay your graduation.

3. Choose committee members who are supportive of your work.

4. Create a support group within your college. I had the privilege of joining a group of dedicated women at the University of Texas at Austin. Cinthia Salinas had started a group to prepare for candidacy exams. Then, she extended that idea to a support group for the dissertation. We met once every week and were committed to those meetings. The meetings were not only used as peer debriefing groups (as suggested in Erlandson, Harris, Skipper, & Allen, 1993; Lincoln & Guba, 1985), but they were also used to discuss successes and concerns with the entire dissertation process.

5. Set a defense date and work backwards from that deadline, making sure all paperwork is completed and committee members are aware of what steps you are taking to accomplish your goal. If you are defending in the summer, set the defense date as early as March or April. Consider the fact that some of your committee

Talk about stress!

Conduct a pilot study as soon as possible.

Think of support groups as a privilege.

Work backwards from a defense date.

members may be out of town during the summer.

6. If you are working, ask your boss for a flexible schedule. If possible, ask to complete some of the work at home.

7. Allow others to help, especially when they can help—e.g., making obvious corrections from committee's feedback, working on bibliography, doing a spell check, etc. If you do not have anyone to help you, leave the more tedious tasks of writing (e.g., table of contents, bibliography) for the part of the day in which you feel less productive writing main parts of your dissertation.

8. Choose a place where you can work. My husband and I worked at a computer lab where I had no distractions, except when we took five-minute breaks to dance to Juan Luis Guerra. Take breaks!

9. Stay in contact with your committee members during the process by sending e-mail to let them know about the status of your dissertation.

10. If you are conducting a qualitative study, be patient during data collection. There will be times when things do not turn out as planned.

Reference:
Erlandson, D. A., Harris, E. L., Skipper, B. L., & Allen, S. D. (1993). *Doing naturalistic inquiry: A guide to methods*. Newbury Park, CA: Sage.

Notes

_____

_____

_____

_____

Contribution 70
Charles L. Madison
Washington State University

Master's degree students had difficulty developing a strong rationale for their project or thesis proposals. The jump from reading the literature in the area of their choice, and the writing of the first draft of their review of literature (with questions or hypotheses) was a

Allow others to help.

Take breaks and dance to the music.

particular problem. I developed the following worksheets that seem to have been successful in helping the students develop their thinking and build a stronger case for their study. The worksheets are turned in as an assignment following the submission of 5–10 article abstracts completed on articles in their topic area, and before they are expected to submit a first draft of their review of literature. Those who find the worksheets useful are welcome to use or modify them to suit their needs.

Project Literature Summary Worksheet

Article (Names/Dates)	Purpose	Subjects	Methods	Results	Conclusions	Comments

Review of Literature Worksheet

The purpose of my project is:
(Give a general statement of purpose.)

Past research in this area has shown that:
(List the major points, including criticism, and note the studies.)

1.

2.

3.

(use additional sheets if needed)

This study is important because:

The major points in my *introduction* and *review of literature* are:
(Be sure to indicate the line of logic you will use to convince others
the study needs to be done.)

1.

2.

3.

4.

5.

(use additional sheets if necessary)

The questions(s) to be answered in this study is (are):
[or the hypothesis(es) to be treated is (are)]

> A worksheet to
> guide in reviewing
> literature.

Contribution 71

Vicki A. Wilson and Linda Morrow
Muskingum College

The following is an assessment rubric designed to help guide our master of arts students in developing and writing their research projects. We began using the rubric just this semester, so we have only anecdotal evidence that it provides helpful direction to our students.

Score	Unsatisfactory	Satisfactory	Exemplary
Length	Less than 20 pages	20 to 30 pages	More than 30 pages
Chapter 1 Introduction	Mismatch between problem and research questions/ hypotheses	Some relationship between problem and research questions/ hypotheses	Clear relationship between problem and research questions/ hypotheses
	Superficial treatment of problem	Adequate treatment of problem; no obvious omissions	Demonstrates clear understanding of problem through inclusion of multiple perspectives and placement of problem in context
	Topic not a substantive one in the field	Topic of documented educational importance	Topic of documented educational importance, well justified
	Missing one or more of the following components: Introduction, rationale for the study, statement of the problem, general hypotheses and/or research questions, definition of terms	All components included	All components included and clearly described

	Unsatisfactory	*Satisfactory*	*Exemplary*
Chapter 2 Literature Review	Fewer than 15 sources	15–20 sources	More than 20 sources
	Includes only opinion and application articles	Includes primarily research and synthesis articles	Includes a variety of high quality sources, including articles from juried publications, interviews, correspondence, etc.; emphasis on research and synthesis articles
	No clear organization	Well organized	Organization pattern demonstrates understanding of prior research on the topic (historical, general to specific, segments of the topics, etc.)

	Unsatisfactory	*Satisfactory*	*Exemplary*
Chapter 3 Methods	Mismatch between research methods and questions/ hypotheses	Uses accepted standards of research methodology	Shows thorough understanding of research methodology used, including assumptions of statistical tests
	No limitations noted	Limitations noted	Thoughtful explanation of limitations and their justification

	Unsatisfactory	*Satisfactory*	*Exemplary*
Chapter 4 Analysis and Results	Inaccurate or incomplete analysis	Adequate analysis	Insightful analysis and interpretation of data
	Lacks adequate narrative description of findings	Includes adequate narrative description of findings	Clear and complete narrative description of findings
	Lacks appropriate charts and/or tables	Tables and charts adequately support written research findings	Tables and charts enhance written research findings

	Unsatisfactory	*Satisfactory*	*Exemplary*
Chapter 5 Summary and Discussion	Lacks summary	Summary adequately covers all components of project	Clear, concise, and thorough summary; publication-quality abstract
	Lacks conclusion or conclusion not supported by the data	Conclusions supported by the data	Insightful conclusions, well supported by the data
	Lacks implications, or implications inconsistent with findings	Includes relevant implications for educators	Includes a variety of implications for relevant audiences: educators, students, parents, etc.
	Limitations not addressed	Superficial treatment of limitations	Insightful treatment of limitations
	Results not tied to literature review	Results tied to literature review	Results compared and contrasted with findings of prior researchers
	Lacks recommendations for future research, or recommendations are inconsistent with findings	Recommendations for future research are consistent with research findings	Thorough exploration of ideas for future research based on the research project

	Unsatisfactory	*Satisfactory*	*Exemplary*
Overall Style/Organization	Contains spelling and grammatical errors	Contains no spelling or grammatical errors	Contains no spelling or grammatical errors, demonstrates creative use of language
	Does not follow APA style	Follows APA style	Conscientiously follows APA style
	Lacks or uses quotations and/or citations ineffectively	Uses quotations and citations appropriately	Uses quotations and citations to enhance written narrative
	Includes sketchy descriptions	Includes adequate descriptions	Uses "thick description" where appropriate
	Organizational plan inconsistent	Organizational plan obvious throughout	Organizational plan enhances project presentation, promotes ease in reading
	Does not maintain focus on research problem		Well written with smooth transitions

Notes:

Notes:

Notes:

Notes:

Notes:

Notes: